DATE DUE

JUL 1 1994			
JUL 2 0 1994			
SEP 6 1994			
JAN 2 8 1995			
OCT 0 1 1996			
JUL 1 6 1997			
MAY 1 1998			
OCT 12 2005			
5/12/09			
GAYLORD			PRINTED IN U.S.A.

John Kruk

with

 Paul Hagen

 SIMON & SCHUSTER
New York London Toronto Sydney Tokyo Singapore

"I Ain't an Athlete, Lady..."

My Well-Rounded Life and Times

SIMON & SCHUSTER
Rockefeller Center
1230 Avenue of the Americas
New York, New York 10020

Designed by Hyun Joo Kim
Manufactured in the United States of America

1   3   5   7   9   10   8   6   4   2

Library of Congress Cataloging-in-Publication Data
Kruk, John, date.
"I ain't an athlete, lady . . ." : my well-rounded life and
times / John Kruk with Paul Hagen.
p.   cm.
1. Kruk, John, date. 2. Baseball players—United States—
Biography. 3. Philadelphia Phillies (Baseball
team) I. Hagen, Paul. II. Title.
GV865.A1K78   1994
796.357'092—dc20
[B]   94-11734
CIP
ISBN: 0-671-89794-2

Photo Credits
San Diego Padres: 4, 5, 6; George Reynolds/Philadelphia
Daily News: 7, 9, 10; AP/Wide World Photos: 8, 11, 13, 14,
15, 16, 17; Rosemary Rahn: 12. All other photographs
courtesy of John Kruk.

To my family, my friends at home—
they know who they are—and
my teammates.
J.K.

To Karen, Emilyanne, and Danby.
P.H.

ACKNOWLEDGMENTS

Just saying thank you doesn't do justice to the contributions of the following people. Without them, this project would never have happened. I will always be grateful to my wife, Karen, for keeping everything else under control; to Emilyanne, ten, and Danby, nine, who understood why their dad spent all off-season holed up in his office; to Dan and Elynor Hagen, who always encouraged their son to read; to Jim and Jo Ann Webb, who have pushed me to do a book forever; to Jeff Neuman, my editor at Simon & Schuster, who had the vision to see the possibilities and the patience to guide two rookie authors through it; to Jeremy Solomon, my agent, who got the deal done; and to John Kruk for his time and generosity.

—P.H.

INTRODUCTION

He had been in New York, talking to publishers about the idea that became this book. On the drive back to Philadelphia, he pulled into a rest stop on the New Jersey Turnpike. He was making a phone call when a woman walked past. She was a few steps past him when her head suddenly snapped around.

She pointed at him and screamed, "You're John Kruk!"

Well, yes. He is.

At the All-Star game last July in Baltimore, the writers had their choice of the best players in baseball to interview. They crowded around Kruk, and he had them laughing out loud as they filled their notebooks.

I had heard that when David Letterman made his big move from NBC to CBS, one of the first guests he requested was Kruk. And I watched when he went on in September and I howled along with the studio audience.

I knew that, in my travels around the National League with the Phillies, other reporters seemed more curious about Kruk than anyone else on the team.

But I was slow to catch on. I didn't think too much about it. After all, the Phillies were in first place every day but one last year. The daily drama of the unfolding worst-to-first story was gripping enough. And it wasn't like this team didn't have a full cast of characters.

It didn't really hit me until that cold day in the first week in December. Between meetings with publishers, we were standing on Second Avenue. John was wearing jeans and sneakers, a windbreaker, and an FBI cap. That's pretty nondescript for midtown Manhattan, but suddenly people started stopping, pointing, asking for his autograph.

New Yorkers are supposed to be jaded. And it wasn't like they would have *expected* to find him loitering on the street. But he was recognized, over and over again.

That's when I started to catch on that John had crossed the line from being a career .300 hitter to something bigger. He had become a celebrity, whatever that means. And more than that, it was clear that people just *liked* him.

Since then, I've thought about what makes him unique and why people are drawn to him. One reason, I think, is that at a time when professional athletes are increasingly remote and inaccessible, he comes across as being just folks. Dresses for comfort, not to impress anybody. Doesn't take himself too seriously, as anyone watching him strike out against Randy Johnson in the All-Star game could tell. He has fun. And then there's that body. Millions of people constantly fight the battle of the bulge; how many other three-time All-Stars can most of us relate to?

I recently did a radio show with Jeff Blair, a friend who covers the Montreal Expos. When the host asked him which player he would pay to see play, he didn't hesitate: "John Kruk. Watching him just makes me feel good. It makes me want to say, 'Yes! I'll take a second helping. Yes! Put a little extra mayo on that cheeseburger. Yes! Dessert. Of course.' "

It's difficult for major leaguers to keep their perspective. Kruk, with a strong family background and deep West Virginia roots, has managed to keep his bearings. I remember talking to him during spring training in 1990. He was eligible for arbitration, but instead he accepted a $655,000 offer from the Phillies. It was a relatively modest raise from the $450,000 he had made the year before, and he could almost certainly have made more if he'd played hardball in the negotiations.

I asked him if his agent had been upset.

"Probably," he said, shrugging.

Then why did he do it?

He mentioned a lot of things, but what it came down to was that he was grateful to the Phillies for taking a chance on him and trading for him the year before, and he didn't think it would have been right to try to squeeze the last penny out of them. Besides, his father would have had to work most of a lifetime to earn $655,000.

Disarmingly, he seems to not quite believe that he is considered among the best in his profession.

Despite that casual exterior, he has a fierce desire to win. And those who question his work ethic haven't seen the countless afternoons, hours before the first pitch, when he comes out for early batting practice—and cusses himself loudly when he pops up or hits a weak grounder.

He can sometimes come across as gruff and grumpy. Some nights he stays late in the trainer's room rather than playing Meet the Press. But if he has made an error or struck out or somehow screwed up, he's always there to face the questions.

He has, quietly, established a scholarship fund at Allegany Community College in memory of Skip Cook, the coach who kept the high school baseball program going almost single-handedly when some wanted to cancel it. And he and his wife, Jamie, support Kruk's Kids, a charitable project for underprivileged youth.

He's basically a real person who just happens to play baseball for a living. People relate to him. Heck, he's the kind of guy you might just run into at a rest stop on the Jersey Turnpike.

Paul Hagen
February 1994

"I Ain't an Athlete, Lady..."

If you have to die, it might as well be a sudden death.

WE WERE ON THE PLANE, FLYING BACK TO

Toronto to continue the World Series, when most of us heard the news.

The Blue Jays were ahead, three games to two. They only needed one more game to win the whole thing. They had the day off. We had to win two games up there. We also had a damn workout scheduled at SkyDome after we landed. Nobody really wanted to go; we figured we needed the rest more. I mean, if you can't hit by that point of the season, you can't hit.

So when Mitch Williams started saying he wasn't going to the stadium with the rest of us, it didn't go over too well. Guys were saying, "The hell you aren't. You're part of this team, too."

Then we found out why he was acting that way. The Phillies had gotten a couple calls from people saying they were going to shoot Mitch because he had blown a save in that wild Game 4 back at Veterans Stadium when we had a five-run lead going into the eighth inning and ended up losing.

As it turned out, the worst that happened was that some idiots threw eggs at his house. But it's scary. You never know. Maybe somebody bet their last three paychecks on you to win. Mitch hadn't gotten much sleep. When we found out why he didn't want to go, we all agreed it was the best thing for him to stay back at the hotel.

Besides, Mitch was just being a team man. He didn't want anyone getting hit with a stray bullet.

Naturally it attracted a lot of attention when he didn't show up that afternoon. But that was nothing compared to the commotion the following night when he came in to try for a save in the bottom of the ninth and instead allowed the three-run homer to Joe Carter that gave the Blue Jays an 8–7 win and their second straight world championship.

Even now it's hard for me to think about what happened.

The Phillies had such a great season. We had a bunch of guys who busted their asses all year. We had fun playing baseball the way it's supposed to be played. It wasn't supposed to end that way.

Somewhere along the way we got this image. We were wild and crazy. The Beasts of the Northeast. Gypsies, tramps, and thieves. We didn't cut our hair and we didn't shave and we didn't take showers. We dressed like slobs. We had personalities: Lenny Dykstra, Dude, with his cheek stuffed full of tobacco and the juice dribbling down his chin. Mitch, the Wild Thing. Curt Schilling, putting a towel over his head on the bench when Mitch pitched. Darren Daulton. Catchers aren't supposed to look that good . . . or hit that well. Dave Hollins, the third baseman so intense that his teammates know to stay away when he gets that look in his eye. Larry Andersen, the reliever with a funny line for every occasion.

The media made a big thing out of it. It was funny, really. We were pretty much the same way the year before, but we sucked, so nobody noticed.

Then we got off to a great start in 1993. We were in first place every day but one during the regular season. We had four guys on the National League All-Star team. We beat the Braves, the team a lot of people thought was the best in baseball, in the playoffs.

Like Darren said, it was a helluva ride.

But the World Series, I don't know. We dreamed so much about getting there and then it was kind of a letdown—not because we lost, but because things changed. We played the same card games and we talked the same trash, but no matter how hard we tried to keep everything the same, it was different.

There were people everywhere—newspaper reporters, radio people, TV cameras. The clubhouse was off limits, but it seemed like there were always people from the league coming in and asking us to go outside and do stuff. That kind of goes with the territory, but it made the series seem more like a business, more commercial. There were a lot of people around during the playoffs, too, but you're more prepared for the playoffs because you're at least playing against a team in your league, a team you've played against twelve times during the regular season, so you know all their pitchers and what they throw. And then you're in the World Series and you're going against a team you haven't really followed and it's a short series and you're kind of unprepared.

You could tell it was different. You'd see guys coming in wearing nice clothes, not your basic jeans and T-shirts. And it wasn't even a travel day.

Jim Fregosi, our manager, played cards with us a lot during the season, but in the postseason he didn't play with us that much because he had to talk to the media and meet a guy here and meet a guy there. And the crowds were different. In Atlanta, during the playoffs, the fans did the tomahawk chop, which we'd kind of gotten used to. They also started another chant—"*Whoot!* There it is!"—every time the Braves did something. I think it was from a rap song. The fans in Philadelphia picked up on it right away. And I guess another difference was a little nervousness or excitement or whatever. We were all a little more subdued because we knew it could end at any time.

It's kind of weird playing an important game in a stadium you don't know. And SkyDome is an interesting building. The greatest thing about it is that there's a McDonald's right inside. A lot of places, you send the clubhouse kid out for a couple burgers, it could take a half an hour; there, he's back in five minutes.

It's got that Hard Rock Cafe. And the hotel windows. Yeah, we all looked to see if we could figure out which room it was that the couple was spotted going at it a few years ago. But once the game starts, you kind of forget about all that stuff.

One thing that makes that place unique is that it's a dome that can be opened or closed. Montreal's is supposed to do the same thing, only twenty years and millions of dollars later it still doesn't work, so now they just leave it shut all the time. Which is fine with me.

They had decided, even before the World Series, to leave SkyDome closed no matter what the weather was like. I know some people would have preferred to play in an open-air stadium if possible, but not me. If you have a dome, why not use it? That's what I think.

Before the first game of the World Series, a couple of our guys almost got into a fight. You have to understand, that's not as unusual as most people probably think; on any team, there are going to be more fights between yourselves than with the other team. You're around each other so much in the clubhouse and on the planes and in the hotels and restaurants and bars that it's bound to happen. But this one was really silly. One of the younger guys changed the music on the CD player in the clubhouse, and one of the older guys wanted to fight him about it. Heck, during the season if somebody wanted to change the music, they changed it. The starting pitcher might get to listen to pretty much whatever he wanted, but somebody usually changed it as soon as he left the room.

And then there we were, in the World Series, and Game 1 started and Pete Incaviglia wasn't on the bench where he belonged. He was up in the clubhouse instead of being with the rest of us, because he was upset about not starting.

The Blue Jays pitched Juan Guzman, a tough right-hander. Inky had had an outstanding year; he was really a team guy who did whatever they asked him, and a lot of times what they asked him to do was sit against tough right-handers so they could start Milt Thompson instead. It had worked pretty well all year. And that was exactly what they did when they put up the lineup for Game 1.

This time, though, Inky didn't like it. And a few of us, a bunch of us, thought it wasn't an opportune time not to be part of the team. He kind of alienated himself from a lot of the team.

I figure it was either selfishness or pride on Inky's part. I'd like to think it was a matter of pride. The man wanted to play. He had played for eight years in the big leagues, same as me, to get to the series for the first time, and you can't blame him for wanting to play. At the same time, it was kind of demoralizing. We went through the whole season as a team and then we got to the point where we were playing for all the marbles and suddenly we had a guy who wasn't on the same wavelength as everybody else. It was tough to understand what was going on. It was tough to understand. If Ricky Jordan had been 20 for 20, he would have been playing first base instead of me. If he's hitting the ball that well, you've got to accept it.

I just don't think Inky handled it the way he should have. It didn't cause us to lose any games, but it showed that he was taking things differently than he had during the regular season.

Guzman was tough, but we did what we wanted to do. We made him throw a lot of pitches. I think that showed something about our team: except for Lenny Dykstra and Mariano Duncan, it was the first time in the World Series for most of us, but we were still able to be patient at the plate.

What really made our offense work all year was that we weren't afraid to take a walk. In other years I would swing at something—anything close they threw at me—if I thought I could drive in a run, even if it meant making an out, because I didn't feel that confident about the guys who were hitting behind me. But this year we looked at our lineup and saw how solid it was and so we all took walks.

We carried that approach into the World Series, and it worked. We scored four runs off Guzman and got him out of the game after five innings. Our scouting reports had said that if we could get to their bullpen we could score more runs. It didn't work out that way, but we did what we were trying to do.

I don't think we ever sat around and talked about it, but we had guys who'd been around awhile. We watched the American League playoffs, and we saw how the White Sox were swinging at whatever the Blue Jays threw up there—a lot of pitches in the dirt, a lot of pitches over their heads. So we went up there wanting to make their starting pitchers work, get a few walks, get the pitch count up, and hopefully get him out of there.

Which we did. But Al Leiter and Duane Ward came in, and we only got one run in the last four innings. Curt Schilling started for us; he didn't pitch his best game and Toronto ended up winning, 8–5.

I had three hits and a walk and scored a couple runs. Had an RBI, too, but just like it was all year, that didn't matter much to me, because we lost the game.

In fact, the at bat I remember most from that game was the one in the sixth, and I remember it because I took a whiff. Struck out with the bases loaded and two outs against Al Leiter. Got me on a slider. He said it was a fastball, but I would have sworn it was a slider. Maybe that's how hitters are—we don't want to admit the pitcher can throw a fastball by us.

I didn't do a thing with bases loaded last year. Somebody told me I was 1 for 13 with bases loaded, but I think that must be wrong. I can't remember the hit.

It got to the point where any time I came up with two guys on, I was hoping they'd get a hit into the gap, because it got depressing after a while. I was aware of it because everybody kept bringing it up. You don't think anybody ever said, "You know, if you had just hit .500 with the bases loaded you'd have had ten or twelve more RBIs than what you had?" No, nobody on our team would bust a guy like that.

I just really sucked with the bases loaded. Which was strange, because hitting with the bases loaded had never been a problem for me in the past. I mean, that's the easiest time to hit. The pitcher can't walk you. If he gets behind in the count he has to give you something to hit. But I just didn't do it. Must have been too easy.

It didn't take a rocket scientist to figure out how important

Game 2 was. We didn't want to come home down two games to none. And we didn't. Terry Mulholland gave up a two-run homer to Joe Carter in the fourth inning, but by then we had scored five in the third against Dave Stewart on only three hits. The rally started with walks to Lenny Dykstra and Mariano Duncan.

Again, we made a starter throw a lot of pitches. Stewart left the game after six. Again, we only got one run against their bullpen the rest of the way. But we had enough to win, 6–4, and go back to Veterans Stadium even.

People probably don't remember this, but Mitch Williams pitched one and two-thirds innings of relief and got the save at a time when the bullpen was pretty worn out.

When you think about playing in the World Series, you don't think about rain, but that was exactly what we got for Game 3. The games start so late anyway, and then we had to wait over an hour because of rain.

It wasn't worth the wait. We got our butts kicked.

You try to handle a rain delay in the Series the same as you would during the regular season, but you can't. During the regular season you play so many games, so who gives a damn? If it gets rained out, it gets rained out. But during the World Series, you're really anxious to get going.

Danny Jackson started for us in Game 3. He went down to the bullpen to warm up, and then the rains came, so he came back. He had to sit awhile and then warm up again. This isn't an excuse, but I think he's the kind of guy who, when he warms up, you have to get him out there. He's real intense. If you could see how much he stretches and the kind of preparation he does, you'd know there's a chance he might have tightened up a little bit. So I don't think that rain delay helped him a lot.

Anyway, he gave up four runs in five innings. Ben Rivera, who had been used as a starter most of the season but was in the bullpen for the postseason, came in and got lit up; the Blue

Jays got four more runs in one and two-thirds innings against him. We didn't do much against Pat Hentgen, and Toronto won easily, 10–3.

Then came one of the strangest games in World Series history, a game that turned out to be the beginning of the end for Mitch.

The Blue Jays got three in the top of the first against Tommy Greene. We came back with four against Todd Stottlemyre in the bottom of the inning. And that's pretty much the way it went for the rest of the night.

Lenny Dykstra hit a two-run homer in the second inning and we were ahead, 6–3. Then the Blue Jays knocked Greene out of the game in the top of the third. They ended up scoring four to go ahead, 7–6.

We tied it up in the fourth. Then we scored five more in the fifth and we were ahead, 12–7. Lenny hit his second home run of the game and scored for the fourth time. And it was only the fifth inning.

Paul Molitor got on base one time—it's hard to remember exactly when; it seemed like it was the eighth time he was on base that night. Anyway, he was on first base and I said to him, "This is like a damn spring training game."

And he says, "No shit. We should be seeing palm trees and either playing in Clearwater or Dunedin and out eating by now."

I said, "This ain't a World Series. The World Series is supposed to be the two best teams in the world playing. And this is not the two best teams in the world right now. I mean, you could go to Williamsport and get two Little League teams to play better than we're playing tonight."

You knew it was going to be an offensive series, and that game sort of epitomized that. It sucked. It was a worthless game. But for people who like excitement, I guess that was the one.

Baseball is funny like that. Sure, there are some blowouts.

But it seems like usually if one team scores a lot of runs, the other team does, too. Or it's a low-scoring game by both teams.

I think that's the athlete's mentality: no matter how far you're down, you always think you can come back. That's even the way we live. If something bad happens, well, no matter what it is, you come back.

We went into the eighth with a 14–9 lead. My first thought was that that should be pretty safe. Then the little man in the back of my head said, "Maybe not. They have a great offense, too."

Still, that game should have been over. I don't care if it's the 1927 Yankees over there; if you lead by five runs and it's the eighth inning, the game should be over. But it didn't happen that way.

Larry Andersen started the eighth, his second inning of work. He was dead tired by that time of the year. Hell, he had a right to be. He was forty years old and had pitched in almost seventy games by that time. But our whole bullpen was tired, so Fregosi had to try to extend Andersen as long as he could. He'd had a 1-2-3 seventh, and he started the eighth by getting Roberto Alomar to ground out, but then he ran out of gas. Joe Carter singled. John Olerud walked. Then came a play that might have turned the game around.

Molitor hit a high hopper toward third base that caught Dave Hollins between hops. He kept moving back on the ball, and finally it bounced past him for a double. Carter scored, Molitor went all the way to second, and after that, nothing went right.

Mitch Williams came in to relieve Andy. This time he had nothing on the ball. Tony Fernandez singled to score Olerud. Now the score was 14–11. Pat Borders walked to load the bases with one out.

At that point Toronto's manager, Cito Gaston, made an

interesting decision: the pitcher, Tony Castillo, was up—and Gaston let him bat. Castillo struck out.

But Rickey Henderson singled and Devon White tripled and that was it: 15–14. The Blue Jays won on a late touchdown.

That was devastating. We came into the clubhouse, and nobody said anything for a half hour, forty-five minutes. Except for the interviews we had to do, nobody said a word.

We were one loss away from the season being over, down three games to one. We had lost two in a row at home. Our bullpen was a mess. And then, like out of nowhere, Lenny Dykstra hollered, "Fuck it. We've just gotta win tomorrow."

It was just like something he'd said during the season. He must've said it ten times: "If we're ever going to get a well-pitched game, now is the time." And it seemed like we usually did, and as we'd be walking off the field, he'd say, "I guess that bastard was listening to me."

Well, thank God that Curt Schilling must have been listening to him that night, because he went out in Game 5 and he pitched his ass off. We got two runs early off Guzman, and Schill made them stand up. He pitched a five-hit shutout when we needed it most. We won, 2–0, and we were still alive.

I was lucky enough to drive in our first run in the bottom of the first. Lenny Dykstra was on third with one out, so I was just trying to get a fly ball, a ground ball, something, it didn't matter what. Just get my bat on the ball. Against Juan Guzman, that's tough enough, so I was happy to ground out to second. Lenny scored and, as it turned out, that was enough for Schill.

For the first seven innings, the Blue Jays only got one runner past first base, but you could tell that Schilling was getting tired. In the seventh, you could start to see his legs weren't as firm under him as you'd like. Sure enough, he gave up two hits to lead off the eighth.

But you have to give Jim Fregosi a lot of credit. Everybody

could see that Schill was out of gas. But so what? If his arm fell off, they could sew it back on and he'd still be ready to pitch again in the spring. So we didn't give a damn. We just wanted him to finish that game. The bullpen was shot; if Schilling could finish, the relievers would get two full days off.

At the end of the eighth inning I went back to the dugout and gave him a little inspirational speech, something like, "Look, dammit, you're not tired. If you think you're tired, you're crazy, because you're finishing this mother." Something along those lines. Your basic Knute Rockne.

Now we were going back to Toronto. We stayed in the clubhouse for quite a while after the game. By the time I went to the parking lot it must have been two or three o'clock in the morning, and wouldn't you know I ran into four, five, six of my friends from home. Well, we started talking. We had a couple beers. One thing led to another. And before I knew it, the sun was up. I realized I had to go back to the hotel and pack and go catch the plane to Toronto.

It was no big deal; I didn't have to be at my best for the workout. But when I got back to the hotel my wife, Jamie, was kind of pissed. I just looked at her and said the only thing I could think of: "*Whoot!* Here I am."

She didn't think it was funny, but anyway, I had a better evening than Mitch did. That was the night he woke up and found the police in his yard. When he asked them what the hell they were doing there, they told him about the death threats. He didn't get any more sleep than I did.

Then again, he didn't have to go to the workout.

It says on the tickets that the World Series goes seven games. That's kind of what you promise people. Well, we wanted to get to the seventh game. And I thought we were going to.

Terry Mulholland started for us, and the Blue Jays got three runs in the bottom of the first. Going into the seventh inning we were behind, 5–1. This team hadn't quit all year, though, and we didn't quit now. We batted around in the seventh and scored five runs. Lenny Dykstra, who was just amazing in the postseason, hit a three-run homer that put us back in the game. We were ahead by one. We were still ahead by one going into the ninth.

It's going to go down in history that Mitch blew the game, that he gave up the home run to Joe Carter and that the loss was his fault. And somebody must have thought that, because six weeks later he was traded to Houston.

But it's not that simple. You have to go back to the eighth inning. That's when it all started to go wrong.

Roger Mason started the inning by getting Joe Carter to fly out to left. Carter was the seventh straight batter he'd gotten out. But Fregosi came to the mound and took him out of the game, bringing in David West. Hindsight is a beautiful thing. Mason was really pitching well, and we were kind of hoping that Fregosi would leave him in. There have been times when he's come out to make a pitching change and Darren and I have actually argued with him right on the field. But not this time. John Olerud was the batter, a left-handed hitter who had batted .370 or something, so Fregosi had to make the move. Westy throws hard, and he'd done the job for us for the better part of the year. He was having a tough series, but you have to hope he can do it one more time. If he pitches Olerud tough, it's a whole different ball game because then there's a good chance they have the bottom of the order coming up in the next inning.

But West walked Olerud. So now Fregosi had to bring in Larry Andersen to face Roberto Alomar. And you could see that Andy was just gassed. He was sweating and struggling. He got Alomar, but he hit Tony Fernandez with a pitch and walked Ed Sprague to load the bases before he finally got out of the inning when Pat Borders popped up. But now, instead of Mitch coming in to face the seven, eight, and nine hitters in the ninth, he was facing the top of the order.

Rickey Henderson was leading off, and of course Mitch

walked him. It's not unusual for Mitch to walk the first guy and get out of it, but this is Rickey Henderson. It's like walking Lenny Dykstra or Otis Nixon when we played Atlanta. It's almost the same as giving them a double because they run so well.

All I was thinking was that if Henderson tried to steal, I hoped he'd slip.

We had heard that he had leg problems and he might not run, and he didn't. But we knew we couldn't count on a double play, either. He could still move. Mitch doesn't get that many ground balls. And Devon White was the batter and he can run, too, so unless he hit a rocket right at someone, it wasn't going to be a double play.

The best we could hope for was to keep Rickey close at first and get Devon White out and take our chances from there. That part worked out. He flied out to left. But now Molitor was up and he was just as hot as Lenny. He singled to put runners on first and second.

Now, Mitch was having a lot of problems late in the year with guys stealing third off him. So he was really concentrating on keeping Henderson close. If there's one thing I regret, looking back on it, it's that I didn't go out to the mound and tell him to quit using the slide step delivery. When you use it, you lose some velocity. See, Mitch has a real high leg kick, so what he was trying to do was not raise his leg much at all, almost like he was just playing catch with Darren. The way he usually pitches, he turns his whole body, and his leg is way up in the air so it's tough for the hitter to pick up the ball when he throws it. But when he shortened up, he not only lost velocity but he gave the hitter a longer look at the ball.

That's the one thing I'd like to change. I wish I had gone in and told him, "If he wants to steal, let him go. But don't lose what you have by trying to change your delivery just to try to keep the guy on base."

If Rickey steals third and Molitor steals second and Mitch has good stuff and gets the next batter, Joe Carter, the steal means nothing. Olerud is already out of the game; Alfredo Griffin had come in to run for him in the eighth and stayed in the game. So if Mitch gets Carter, we still have a good chance to win.

But he went with the slide step. He was trying to get the pitch up and away, but it was down and in. It wasn't a horrible pitch. But Joe Carter gets paid a lot of money to hit home runs, and he just happened to pick the wrong time to hit one. I guess it was the right time for him.

I went numb.

It wasn't like the end of any other season. Let's face it, in most other seasons we couldn't wait for the last game to end so we could get the hell out of there and go home.

As it was, though, I woke up the next morning and my first thought was that I had to get up and go to the stadium. And then it hit me that there wasn't a game, that the season was over. It was still kind of a shock. I got on the plane to go back to Philly and it was still hard to believe. There was nothing. Nothing we could say, nothing we could do. It was over.

I have a lot of blanks about what happened right after the sixth game. I remember walking off the field and going down the steps into the dugout. I remember all the photographers there and one of them yelling, "Go the fuck home, you fuckin' hoodlums." Something like that. And if it had been the regular season I would have wanted to grab him and jerk him out of there and kick the shit out of him. I wanted to tell him to go fuck himself. But what's the point? So I just walked in, numb, and I wasn't really thinking about anything.

I didn't want to kill Mitch. I didn't want to kill Joe Carter. There was nothing. It was just eerie. Usually after a game we'd sit around and have a few beers and talk about what we had to do to help us win. But we couldn't even do that because

there were no more games. It was depressing. It felt like we'd
died. It's hard to explain. It's like you have a favorite pet, a
dog, and you can't wait to get up every morning to play with
your dog. You look forward to it. And then one day the dog
dies and it's over.

There were no tears shed—not by the players, anyway. Bill
Giles, the owner, came in. He told us we had nothing to be
ashamed of, that we shouldn't feel bad. And then he started
bawling.

A long time after the game was over a few of the Toronto
players came over to our clubhouse—Dave Stewart, Duane
Ward. We hung out for a while. That was cool. But then you
get up in the morning and get dressed, and you realize you're
not getting dressed to go to the ballpark. You're getting dressed
to go home and it's all over.

When we landed in Philadelphia there were a lot of people
there to meet us, and that helped remind us that we'd had a
pretty good year after all. I think what we did was special. We
captured a city like I don't think any team in Philadelphia had
ever done before. We had players the fans could identify with.

We did what we did and we said what we said. Most of us
didn't kiss ass, and I think the people in Philadelphia appreciated that because they're tough people. They live their lives
there and they don't take shit from nobody. That's the way we
played the season, just like our fans live. It's not that we consciously tried to be like them. It's just the way we were. But a
lot of us could have grown up in Philly.

We never asked them to like us. But we didn't take shit. We
just played our game and went about our business. If something happened, we dealt with it in our own way. Just like
Philadelphia. And when you score a lot of runs and have Mitch
as your closer, you know it has a chance to be exciting every
day. And they came out to watch.

People asked me a lot during the postseason how it felt to

be in a sudden death situation. And I always said that if you have to die, it might as well be a sudden death. In the playoffs, when the Braves beat us, they blew us out, but so what? Games like that are easier to deal with. It's like, would you rather get shot a hundred times with a BB gun or once with a .357?

In the end, that one stray bullet from the .357 got us after all.

If you called somebody a psychopathic idiot, it was a pretty good compliment.

THE PHILLIES HAVE THIS IMAGE OF BEING

some kind of out-of-control group of freaks. You know, they lock us up in a cage after each game and throw us some red meat. That kind of thing.

But that's just an image. You know that tennis player, the one who says image is everything? Well, that's bullshit. And anyway, what do tennis players know? Before they can play, everybody has to be quiet. I don't get it. Can you imagine what would happen if it's the bottom of the ninth and the bases are loaded and all of a sudden we stop the game and ask everybody to be quiet so we can concentrate on our hitting?

Sure, we had fun. If you weren't careful, you might get a pie in the face, especially while you were doing a television interview. But we weren't bad. We didn't hurt anybody. If we were going to hurt somebody, it would probably be ourselves.

We horsed around. My back bothered me most of the year and I said something to Pete Incaviglia, probably that he was a dumb Italian or something innocent like that, and he came over and picked me up from behind, bad back and all, and I thought he was going to crush me. I thought he was going to throw me into a locker. I'd have done the same thing if I was him.

All in good fun.

When I was traded from San Diego to the Phillies in June 1989, it was a totally different situation. There were some people in the front office who didn't want any personalities at all. Once I even got benched because I said a bad word coming back to the dugout after I made an out.

Isn't it funny how things are? When we sucked, it was, "You're a bad boy. You're going to be punished." Then we were in first place and they decided, "Oh, we can market that. Look at how colorful we are. We have a band of renegades, but they can play baseball. We can work with this." I mean, when we were dead last we were assholes; when we were in first place we were trendsetters. When we lost, nobody wanted to hear about it; when we won, it was a great story. And all the time we stayed the same, drinking beer and cursing, wearing long hair and beards. Somebody even put out a T-shirt with me and Lenny Dykstra and Darren Daulton on the front and "The Wild Bunch" written under our pictures. I guess people thought we were okay once they figured out they could make some money off us.

By the way, we didn't get any of that money.

As I was saying, though, things were a lot different when I first got to the Phillies. I was ready to leave San Diego. I was happy when the front office called me in and told me that Randy Ready and I had been traded to Philly for Chris James. We both were. We were in Cincinnati and we were in the showers and naked and hugging. The other players must have been wondering.

The next morning Randy and I got up and flew to Philadelphia. We were all excited. We got there early, about noon. And we went straight from the airport to the clubhouse. We walked in . . . and there was no one there, just the guys who work there.

We thought, Well, maybe there isn't a game tonight. That would explain it. We had nowhere else to go, so we stayed at the clubhouse. Then, around three of four in the afternoon, players started rolling in. But nobody came up and said, "Glad to have you." Nothing. None of the normal bullshit that you say to players when they get traded.

I couldn't believe it. I was so happy to be traded. I was thinking it was a new start on life. I was only hitting a buck eighty, I wasn't in a good situation, I was happy to be coming back to the East Coast. And then it was like, Jesus Christ, this might be the same shit I just left. Jesus Christ, they sent me to a morgue.

It was like this was the place they sent everyone to die. Nobody wanted to be there. Going to the ballpark every day was like going to a funeral; you didn't want to go, but you knew you had to. I told Randy, "We're going to have fun. Just because they're miserable doesn't mean we have to be miserable, too."

Larry Bowa, who had been my manager in San Diego and was now the Phillies third base coach, talked to me. He said, "Man, just be yourself. Have fun. We've got a bunch of deadasses here, but don't let them bring you down. Just go out and have fun. Play your game. And don't worry about the bullshit that goes on here, because you're going to see some stuff you've never seen before. Guys pouting and not caring if we win or lose as long as they get a couple hits."

He was right. Later that year we called a kid up from the minors. And Tommy Herr, who was the second baseman at the time, goes over to him and says, "Grab a bucket and start bailing." Like, welcome to a sinking ship. I couldn't believe that attitude.

Sure, I noticed that the guys were like that. But I'd had a bad year the season before and I was having a *really* horseshit year when I got traded. I said to myself, Man, if I have another bad year I'm going to get released. Because that would be two bad years in a row and not many people are going to take a chance on somebody who's had two bad years in a row.

I decided right then that if I was going to get released, I would enjoy the hell out of my last season, because I might never get a chance to play ball again. I just said to hell with it. And I started to hit.

Pretty soon after that things started to get better because the general manager, Lee Thomas, didn't like what was going on any better than we did. He started bringing in people who were worse than me. And I thought, This ain't going to be bad after all.

It was just a little over two weeks after I was traded to the Phillies, a Father's Day game at the Vet, when it started. Lee traded our second baseman, Juan Samuel, to the Mets for Lenny Dykstra and Roger McDowell. When we got Roger, I knew that was it. That was stretching the limit of sanity about as far as it can go. He's a different breed. One of the first things he did was put an aquarium over his locker with his pet snake in it.

We still weren't winning many games, but it was nice to see that they wanted people in here who had fun and enjoyed themselves, then went out and played hard. That's the way Roger was; he had fun, but when he got the ball he pitched his ass off.

That's the way it should be. And after a while the other guys started following suit. Even Darren Daulton started breaking out a little. No more Mr. Businessman, three-piece suit, bring your briefcase to the ballpark.

Of course, if I looked like Darren I might dress that way, too. As it is, I just try to cover myself up with as much denim as possible.

Now we have this team with some, shall we say, unusual types. And it starts right from the top.

When Lee Thomas was a player his nickname was Mad Dog and he didn't get that for nothing. He's got a temper. A couple years ago somebody asked him if he wanted to play golf. He said he couldn't, and opened the trunk of his car: all his clubs were broken in two. The man goes through a bunch of golf clubs in a year.

Two years ago things weren't going too well. Lee called three or four of us up to his office for a meeting. We were talking about different things, and then he and Mitch Williams started to go at it. It was like watching two little kids. I thought they were going to fight.

My first spring training with Philadelphia, Lee had a club-house meeting about how we should watch our language on the field. And all the time he was telling us not to curse, he was saying "Fuck this" and "Fuck that." Roger McDowell counted twenty-three "fucks" in a meeting that lasted less than three minutes.

I think Lee called the meeting for the benefit of Nick Leyva, who was the manager back then. Nick had said something to me about watching my language and Lee felt he had to stand behind his manager, but the way he did it showed the players that he was more attuned to us than he was to that choirboy image we were supposed to have.

We don't have a choirboy image. Not anymore.

And, yeah, Lee got a pie in the face before a game.

There ought to be a clause somewhere that says if you're going to play for the Phillies, you have to be thick-skinned, because you're going to get some abuse. I mean, we abused Dale Murphy. From the outside looking in, people probably thought we were the biggest bunch of assholes, because I don't think there's anybody in the history of the game who is held in higher esteem than Dale Murphy.

The thing is, I think Murf enjoyed being treated like one of the guys after all those years in Atlanta where everybody tip-toed around him. People also didn't realize that when it came right down to it, he had a wicked tongue on him. It wasn't nasty, it was just wicked. He could bring you down and put you in your place as quick as anybody.

He was wise.

For example, if one of our pitchers doesn't pitch good, I might just call him a fuckin' pussy or something like that. Murf had a way of getting his point across without saying a bad word, but the point was made and it hurt worse than if somebody else had cursed you, because you really had to stop and think about what he'd said. If somebody calls you a fuckin' pussy, there ain't but one thing you can do.

But with Murf, he'd say something. Then after he walked away you'd start thinking about it. And you'd realize, Man, he was mad at me. He might say something like, "You know, I don't think you did as well as you could have. I think you really didn't bear down and do quite the job you were expected to do." That was all. But then you'd start thinking about what your job was and what you should have done and you'd really feel bad, because he was the last guy in the world you'd want to let down.

I was sorry that he couldn't have been with us when we won. We had to let him go right at the end of spring training. He signed with the Colorado Rockies, but retired by the end of May. I guess Murf's one of those guys who was just cursed. First he was with the Braves all those years, then right after they trade him they go to the World Series two straight years; then he comes to us when we suck, and the year we let him go, we make it there. If the Rockies win it all this year, you'll know for sure something weird's going on.

Murf was definitely part of the team, even though he was so different from the rest of us. Once I said our team was one Mormon and twenty-four morons. Another time there was a rumor that the customs officials going into Canada were going to detain shady characters, so I told the writers I hoped Murf could play all nine positions.

We got on him, though, just like we get on everybody. And one time I pushed him too far.

We had just played a getaway day game in Chicago, and the bus ride from Wrigley Field to the airport always takes a long time because of all the traffic. We won that day but Murf struck out two or three times, once on a really bad pitch. Now, he doesn't say much, but he got a little upset after one of the strikeouts, and he threw his bat a little. The grass was kind of damp and the bat skipped. I was on deck and I had to jump over it.

When somebody throws a bat at you, even if it's not on purpose, it could injure you. I didn't want to say anything right then, because he was upset. I waited until after the game when we got on the bus. Murf was sitting there, reading the paper and doing his crossword puzzle like he always did. And I started to get on him a little bit.

We were going to be off the next day, and I was having a couple beers and I said something about him having such a good day that day. He just kind of gave me a little glance that he can give. When he does, it means shut up, but I didn't want to. I wanted to keep going. I thought I could get on a roll with him, so I kept going.

A little farther down the road I said something else to him. Probably something clever like, "You sucked today" or "What the hell were you doing?" I might have even said, "What's the matter, were you out too late?"

Well, he never goes out at all, so you knew he wasn't out too late. He kind of told me to shut up then. I said, "What are you going to do? Come back and hit me?" And he told me, "Shut up or I'm going to bop you one."

In normal language that means, "You'd better shut the fuck up or I'm going to come over there and beat the shit out of you." But Murf didn't curse. "Bop you one" was his way of saying the same thing.

But I couldn't stop. I said, "What are you going to do, hit me? You couldn't hit a ball all day. Then you tried to throw your bat at me and you couldn't even hit me with that. What are you going to do? If you try to hit me you'll just swing and miss."

He dropped his paper. And when he's doing his crossword puzzle, he ain't going to drop the paper. He threw it on the floor and he started walking back.

I knew then that I might have gone a little too far.

I was thinking, I'm a dead man. He's had eighteen years of never losing his temper, never getting pissed off, and now he's gonna take it all out on me and I'll never, ever see the light of day again.

But he just told me to shut up. And when that man stood up and came to the back of the bus and told me to shut up, I figured there was only one thing I could do.

I started in on somebody else.

You have to understand that I learned from the best, Garry Templeton, when I was in San Diego. He was probably the best all-time shit-talker I've ever heard. Goose Gossage was good, but Tempy was the best. He could talk shit more and worse than anyone.

I sat there and I listened. And I thought, One of these days, I'll be able to do this.

I'll tell you what makes a great trash talker. It's being relentless and not being afraid to say anything to anybody. It doesn't matter who, either—black, white, Latin, whatever. If something happened during a game, Tempy would just go on and on for a whole trip. And he was fun to listen to.

Until he started on you.

Then it was kind of different. You just sat there and were kind of humbled by the whole thing. You know, here's a guy who had a hundred hits from both sides of the plate in the same season. Who was I to say shut up? It was the same thing with Murf. I figured, there's a man with back-to-back Most Valuable Player seasons, so when he said something to me, I knew it really was time to shut up.

The thing is, it's all done for a reason. It breaks the tension. It keeps a guy from dwelling on something he did wrong. You say something in a joking way to make a point. Say a guy strikes out with runners in scoring position and the next guy gets a hit. You might say, "What were you swinging at? Take the walk if they don't throw you a good pitch. I'll drive him in."

The thing about baseball is, you feel bad if you don't do your job in a key situation, and you feel even worse because you think you let your teammates down. So when you get on someone, that's a way of showing the guy that you're still going to speak to him, he's still going to be your teammate and your friend. It's a way of breaking the ice in a fun way.

Our clubhouse has a lot of personalities. We have a lot of guys who can talk some trash. It's the kind of atmosphere where, if you called somebody a psychopathic idiot, it was a pretty good compliment. It meant he fit right in.

Take Lenny Dykstra. He has the locker next to me back in the corner of the clubhouse. Before a game, he's always so hyper, always on the go. He's at his locker. Then he's in the training room. Then he's back at his locker. Then the equipment room. Then the coaches' room. Back to his locker. To the lunchroom. To his locker. Back and forth.

You know, we've lockered next to each other for almost four years, and I don't think we've ever had a real conversation. Like, he'll ask me something about a pitcher and I'll start telling him how the guy worked me, but before I get halfway through it, Lenny's up and gone.

When I was playing against him, I thought he was the biggest asshole in the United States. God, I couldn't stand him. Benito Santiago, when we were in San Diego, said to Lenny one day, "I told our pitchers to drill you every time up because you're such a prick."

But I think to be a great leadoff hitter, that's the way you have to be. And we've got the perfect asshole to lead off for our team. When Dykstra's on your team, you love him. There's not a better guy to play with.

Lenny goes all out all the time, on and off the field. It was devastating in 1991, on the day I was getting married, to find out that he had driven his car into a tree, with Darren Daulton as a passenger. The only thing I'm grateful for is that he wasn't killed. And I hope he learned something from it, which I think he did. I don't think you're going to see him do something like that again. I hope not, anyway.

One thing about Lenny is that he's a lot smarter than people give him credit for. He makes the deals. He knows the people. He's always got something going. If you want to buy something, he always knows somebody to go talk to who will give you a break on the price.

I don't know anybody. I don't take the time. One year I lived near Lenny, and if it hadn't been for him, that house probably would have stayed empty. I wouldn't have known where to go for anything—furniture, TV, any of that stuff. But he knew.

I tested him once. I asked him where to go to get a Christmas tree, and he knew somebody who'd give me a deal on a tree. I couldn't believe it.

Everybody knows how intense Dave Hollins, our third base-man, is. His nickname is Mikey. When he gets this certain look, if it's getting close to game time and somebody asks where Dave is, somebody will say, "Dave's not home right now. Mikey's in." That's his middle name and it's also his alter ego.

I've had fun just watching him, because of the way he plays. The Phillies got him from the Padres organization in the Rule 5 draft, which meant we had to keep him on the major league roster all year. He wasn't playing much, just pinch-hitting, and it was tough on him.

These days, though, if he has four bad at bats, it's a bad night, and he's rough to talk to, or even look at. You don't know if he's going to snap or what. But it was so much worse when he was pinch-hitting. If he made an out he might not get another at bat for a week, and he was miserable. I kept telling him, "Man, there's no way. You're getting one at bat, you're facing a guy who's making great pitches on you, and you're done. You can't expect to get a hit every time up." He just never understood that.

I was happy when they finally let Dave play every day. Otherwise he would have killed somebody, I think.

One time I thought he was going to—kill somebody, I mean. It was 1992, the first spring after we traded Charlie Hayes to the Yankees. He was going to be the third baseman. They pretty much told him that.

We were playing one of the early exhibition games, the kind where the regulars play about five innings, get a couple at bats, run, and leave. Well, Jim Fregosi let me and Lenny go early. Darren Daulton didn't catch at all. But Dave had to play the whole game.

Late in the game he walked past Fregosi in the dugout. He didn't look at him, but he said, loud enough for everybody to hear, "I guess I gotta play nine fuckin' innings every fuckin' day." And then he ran out to his position.

Well, Fregosi didn't say anything. But the next day he made Dave play all nine innings in a B game at ten o'clock in the morning. Then he made him take the trip to St. Petersburg for the regular game. He didn't play, he just sat and watched. And on the way back, Dave was steaming. I mean, he was hot. He told me, "When I get off this bus, I'm going to kick Fregosi's ass. I'm going to kill that motherfucker."

I said, "You can't kill the manager. It don't work."

We got into the clubhouse and we took our stuff off. We got ready to take a shower, and he was still steaming. He just gets that look and you know something is going to happen and it's not going to be very pleasant.

I knew him a little. I didn't know if he'd snap on me or what, but I knew it wouldn't be a good thing for him to kill the manager. He might never play again. So I figured, well, if he hits me instead of Fregosi we can just say that I said something to provoke him and that'll be that. I went up to him and I said, "Hey, you can't kill the manager. I don't care what you do, but you're not going to kill the manager. You've got to calm down." I told him that Fregosi was doing it for a reason. He was being tested. I told him I had been tested like that when I was a young player and Lenny had and Darren had. When you're young, they try to test you and see if you can handle it mentally. And that's one of their tests.

He said, "I don't give a fuck. I'm gonna kill him."

I could see I wasn't getting through to him, so I said, "Let's go get something to eat and we'll sit down and talk about it." And we talked and finally he said all right, he would give Fregosi another chance.

Later in the year Fregosi thanked me for saving his life. He had heard Dave was going to kill him. He wasn't going to call him in and talk to him, because that's not the way it's done, but he said, "I'm glad you talked to him and got him out of there, because I was thinking he was going to come after me."

Like I said, I love to watch the way Dave Hollins plays. He needs to relax a little, though. I know that's the way he's always been and you wish you had a whole team of guys that tough, but sometimes I wish he'd realize it's a game and it's supposed to be fun.

Who knows how long your career is going to last? While it does, you have a chance to talk to a guy like Dale Murphy or Ryne Sandberg. You have a chance to say hi to Barry Bonds, a superstar. But Dave won't mingle. Baseball's not a game to him. It's war. It's us against them. That's the way he is. I've seen guys he played with in the minors, on the other team now, and they try to talk to him, but he won't do it because they're not in his foxhole anymore; they're on the other side, and if they jump out of their hole he's got to try and shoot them. That's his mentality.

Of all the guys on the team, I'm closest to Darren Daulton. It's an Odd Couple thing. He was another guy I didn't like when I played against him. I thought he was just a pretty boy. Something about him rubbed me the wrong way. Even when I first was traded to the Phillies, we didn't hang together. He was too pretty. I thought, Fuck him, let him do his thing.

I figured he didn't like me, either. Even though I do shower and I do wash my hair. I don't know if people realize that or not.

Now, it's true that I'm not a big fan of *combing* my hair. I brush my teeth and all, but combing my hair? That's why I have a lot of hats. But Darren, you look at him at eight o'clock or nine o'clock in the morning before a day game, and it's like he's doing a photo shoot for some fashion magazine. It kind of pisses you off. Catchers are supposed to be all pug-nosed with mangled-up hands. But he can catch and still look the way he does. We're complete opposites, and I figured there was no way this was going to work.

But after a while I realized that, you know, Darren's as much of a dirtball as the rest of us. He just looks better. Underneath, though, he's the same as the rest of us. He's a derelict and he talks shit—and those are beautiful compliments. It's like when Dale Murphy called Lenny Dykstra the little earth pig. I think Lenny appreciated that. Outside of our domain, people have a hard time understanding that. It's like calling Lenny a little asshole; he is, but he's a good little asshole.

That's kind of the way it was with me and Darren. After a while, I realized we had more in common than I thought. I had assumed he was from California, grew up on the beach, had a tan twelve months a year. But I found out he's from Arkansas, he's a farmer, and his nickname is Bubba. So I decided he wasn't that bad a guy after all. (By the way, I have nothing against people from California. But it's tough to get a guy from California to fit into our clubhouse right away. They have their own ideas out there.)

Mariano Duncan fits right in even though outwardly he seems different, mostly because of the way he dresses. I don't think I've ever seen him wear the same clothes twice. His outfits range from outrageous to more outrageous. We kid him that when he opens his closet each morning to pick out his clothes he has to wear sunglasses. He is a colorful human being. I never knew leather came in all those colors, and he has the whole matching outfit right down to the belt and the shoes.

My wife said one day she wished I had clothes like his. I don't think that would work.

But he's another example of a guy who fits right in even though he's different in a lot of ways. Before the Phillies signed Mariano as a free agent prior to the 1992 season, we heard some things about him. We heard that he was selfish and that he would quit on you. We heard that if he wasn't playing well he'd go into his shell and not try to fit in or have a rapport with us.

From the first day, though, he was great. He speaks good English, but he's got that accent and sometimes he says things in the wrong tense. We tease him about it and he laughs, and he fits in great.

Then there's Jim Eisenreich. In some ways, he was a lot like Dale Murphy when he first joined the team. We all knew he had Tourette's syndrome, so we didn't know what to expect. We didn't know if we were going to sit around and watch him shake all the time. I didn't know if we could handle that.

But, just like with Murf, we weren't going to back off. We had a good feeling coming into spring training and we wanted to know what he was made of. If we yelled and cursed at him and he just withdrew, we'd think that when it came time to do or die, we wouldn't be able to depend on him. So I was happy when he started firing back. At that point, I said, "Yeah, we've got a good one here."

I got the feeling from talking to him that the other teams he had been with sort of shied away from him because he had this disease. He fit right in with the Fightin' Phils because we were all kind of hyper. And once he realized we weren't going to let up on him, we weren't going to let him off the hook, we were going to say things that had probably never been said to him before, then I think he understood that it was fun and that we had accepted him.

When you play this game, you fail so many times that you have to expect it. And when you walk into the clubhouse, you expect to get ridiculed. If you walk in and everyone just moves aside and lets you go, it's boring. When we got to Eisie he jumped right into the fray and came back with some good stuff, too.

When he first got to Clearwater last spring, I didn't think he was going to speak. The first day he just sat and stared. He didn't crack a smile. That's when I first thought of calling him Jeffrey Dahmer, because I was looking at him and it seemed

like, my God, he was thinking of all the things he was going to
do to us.

Everybody was walking around saying hello. Then after a
while the usual hell broke loose. The usual exchange of pleas-
antries. "Why didn't you call me all winter, you fat fuck?"
Fuck this and fuck that. We were getting all that out of the
way.

And Eisie just sat there staring.

I said to some of the guys standing there, "Look at that guy.
He doesn't flinch. He looks like a serial killer, staring like he
wants to murder one of us. He looks like Jeffrey Dahmer, just
sitting there at his trial, not blinking."

So I started calling him Dahmer, and he liked it. His wife
came up to me one day in spring training and said she hated
me, hated all of us. At first I thought she was serious. Then she
started laughing and explained how Jim would come home and
keep her up all night telling her stories about the things we had
called him. I mean, how many guys are going to go home and
tell their wives that everybody is calling them Jeffrey Dahmer?
But Eisie seemed to enjoy it, really get into it.

One day he brought a bow and a hunting magazine into the
clubhouse. He said he was going to order some stuff because
he liked to go bow hunting. I told him he couldn't hunt during
baseball season. He said, "I'm not going to hunt any animals.
I'm going to shoot one of you guys." He said something about
eating Darren's leg. I thought, "Wow, this guy is really fucked
up. He'll fit right in."

We made an overnight trip during spring training. He was
rooming with Pete Incaviglia. On the bus back to Clearwater,
Inky said, "Hey, Dahmer, thanks for not eating me last night."
And Eisie says, "You're welcome, Lunch."

I knew then he was one of us.

He had a great year, the best year of his life. He platooned
in right field with Wes Chamberlain. Coming into the year, we

were really worried about Chamberlain. We knew he had potential and power and a chance to put up some good numbers, but we didn't know if he had the desire to do it.

Spring training went pretty good for him. Then we opened the season with three games in Houston. He only started one of the games and he was a little upset, but he talked to Fregosi on the workout day back in Philadelphia. He was told he was going to start the home opener. And then he was late; he showed up about an hour before the game and was scratched from the lineup.

That pissed a lot of people off because there had been questions about him. It was, jeez, here we go with this guy. There was even talk of getting rid of him, sending him the hell out. What really compounded the problem was that it was our home opener and we got killed. That added fuel to the fire.

But he called a team meeting the next day before batting practice, apologized to everyone and promised it wouldn't happen again. And it didn't. From that day on, I think everybody had a lot more respect for him and was a lot friendlier toward him. In past years maybe guys weren't too friendly to him because they didn't know what to expect. But last season he had a real consistent attitude and he topped it off in the World Series; he was one of the first guys there and he was cheering for us just like he was playing and getting three hits every day.

We had another platoon in left with Milt Thompson and Pete Incaviglia. Milt did a nice job for us, and Inky was unbelievable. He hit 24 homers and drove in 89 runs in just 368 at bats. That's practically impossible.

Inky is so strong. Somebody gave him the name Bluto in spring training and it fit. He's a big, barrel-chested guy, always trying to bully people, but deep down he's a softie. He's not as rough around the edges as everybody thinks.

He hit a grand slam off the foul pole in left that would have landed way back in the upper deck. I was on second. As soon as he hit that pitch I knew that if it was fair, it would be a home run, and if it was foul, I'd have to go back. All I could hear was third base coach Larry Bowa: "Tag up. Tag up." Yeah, right. A man from NASA was the only one who needed to tag up on that ball.

Inky just loves to hit. He must wear out the eardrums of Denis Menke, our hitting coach, talking about different stances and different ways of holding his hands. He always has a bat in his hands. One time we were playing a game in Florida and it was twenty minutes before the game and he was in the cage under the stands hitting. It must have been 120 degrees, but he loved to hit.

Then there are the pitchers. They're a different breed to begin with. They're all screwed up; every starting pitcher on every team I've ever been with has been a mess. I think it's because when you play every day, you know that when the game is over you'll get another chance tomorrow, but a starting pitcher, if he doesn't pitch good, has to wait four days, and that has to be hard.

Pitchers are just a different breed. They're like a tick on a dog; they're worthless for four days, but then they have to suck blood on that fifth day.

I mean, what do they do? You can't put them in to pinch-run because you're afraid that if they slide they'll get hurt. Except for a select few, you can't use them to hit. Tommy Greene, Dwight Gooden—there aren't many others I can think of. Omar Olivares, but he played another position in the minor leagues. So for four days the pitchers just sit around. I wouldn't want to do that.

Now, the normal thing in our clubhouse is to rip people, but you don't want to be ripping a guy who has to go try to get people out that night. So it's best that they just stay down at their end of the clubhouse, and mostly they do.

Sometimes they'll stray, though. Tommy Greene comes

down close to where we are, and he takes some abuse from us. Not from the other pitchers, of course; they're like a fraternity. But every once in a while they come down and take some heat and then go back to their end of the clubhouse.

After a game it's okay to have a beer with a pitcher. On days when they don't pitch, it's fine. But on the day they pitch I don't want to be friendly, because in a few hours I might be ripping them. You have to be consistent. You can't be a hypocrite. If you talked to them before the game you'd have to tell them how great they are, build them up. Then after the game, if they got ripped, you'd have to tell them that they sucked. It's just a matter of brutal honesty.

Terry Mulholland was our opening day starter. He was on his own program. He showed up when he wanted to and he did whatever he wanted. That doesn't sit well with some people, but Fregosi has always stressed that we're men, that we should be ourselves. Terry showed up late, but he always showed up late, so he was consistent. Sometimes you get on a plane and you won't see him. But that's just the way he is. He'll be the same way now that he's been traded to the Yankees.

Some guys thought Mulholland got preferential treatment, but it's just that he was in his own world. He does what he wants and doesn't say two words while he's there. But he works hard. He's got such bad knees. You don't see him out on the field during batting practice, and some people might wonder where he is and think he should be out there with the rest of us. But I'd like to see anybody else do what he does on the exercise bike. I don't think they could.

Curt Schilling wants to be one of us, but we won't let him in. Every once in a while we let him sit in on our little debates, but our pitching has been so bad that most of the time we're guarded now. Even when our pitchers pitch good, we wonder if they can keep doing it. If we played for twenty years with a guy and he put up numbers like Steve Carlton, then maybe in his eighteenth or nineteenth year we might decide he was all right.

Don't get me wrong; Schill has done a great job and right now I'd probably have to say he's our best pitcher. But I think sometimes he says too much. He should just worry about his job. We'll worry about the other stuff. When you get a good pitcher, you don't want him to think too much. That's when he gets into trouble.

Last year he lost one game and he said he lost his confidence. With an arm like that? Come on. You can maybe go into a slump, but you don't lose your confidence. He was 7–1 or 8–1 when he made that comment. And he's starting to lose his confidence? That's ridiculous. There are pitchers who would give almost anything to be 7–1 or 8–1 at any point in the season. I think it was just an excuse, because Schill wasn't pitching *that* bad.

That's what I mean when I say I think he talks too much. He's a little immature. He's bounced around a few organizations and I don't think he's ever really been accepted anywhere. He wants to be accepted here, and when you want people to like you, sometimes you do things that are out of character. I mean, we like Schilling. We need him. He has to pitch for us. But to make a comment that you don't have confidence, there's no need for that. We know he's out there doing his best. And that's all we ask.

There are ups and downs. But hitting .300 is up and hitting .200 is down. Being 8–1 isn't down. So it kind of makes you skeptical when you hear a guy talking like that, because then you're not quite sure what to expect from him.

But Schill came back from that in the second half of the season, after Darren Daulton ripped him in the paper. And we had a long talk with him in the weight room. We told him that his pitching was the most important thing. I think he just got caught up in too much stuff. Calling the talk radio shows from his car phone. Having a house built. Here's a guy who was making a million dollars and he builds an $800,000 house and buys a Lamborghini. It just seemed like he had other priorities. Did he really lose confidence in his pitching? Or was he thinking, I'm not pitching good right now and I have an $800,000 house and a $200,000 car and what if I get released? Did he want to pitch good just to make money to pay for those things, or did he want to pitch good to help us win? We didn't know where he was coming from. And I think he kind of admitted that. And after that, he pitched great.

Now, Danny Jackson is a psycho. He's a Dave Hollins who pitches. His nickname is Jason, like in the Friday the 13th movies. On the days he's pitching, you don't want to be near him, because he's on a different level. The other days he's sitting there with his glasses on and you think he's a pretty nice guy. But on the days he's pitching he's a completely different person.

Most people didn't find out about his Pump Us Up act, where he flexes his muscles and rips his shirt and acts like a professional wrestler, until we clinched the National League East in Pittsburgh. When Danny's son came into the clubhouse one day, we asked him, "Can you pump us up like your dad?" He got real shy and hid behind Danny. Then he asked his dad, "Is that the same thing you do at home?" It's a wrestling fetish. I guess they watch a lot of Hulk Hogan.

It seemed like every time he did it, everybody got excited. So what the heck? If it works for him, let him keep doing it. He makes enough money to be able to buy new shirts. He's a real competitor.

The first time Danny did it was early in the year, in June when we played the Mets at Shea Stadium. Mitch Williams struck out the last three batters to end the game. We won, and after the game in the clubhouse Danny peeled his shirt off all of a sudden and started flexing, saying, "Pump us up!" And we were looking at each other like, damn, look at this guy. Then he went out his next start and pitched a shutout. So he just kept doing it.

The other thing you have to know is that he was the only one who did it. Generally if someone starts something, a saying or a fad, it goes around the clubhouse, and pretty soon everybody is doing it. But he was the only guy who ever did that. He was the only guy who had the mentality to do it. Or maybe lack of mentality.

Danny came to us after a couple subpar years, but he had confidence. No matter what his record was, it was like he didn't care if he finished 0–0 as long as the Phillies won. I really think that's the way he approached it. He was excited during every game whether he was pitching or not.

As far as the relievers go, well, I told Larry Andersen at the end of the year that my sole regret in my career so far was that I had only played one year with him. He's a gem, a strange bird. You never know what's going to happen with him, what's going to come out, something funny or something stupid. I had a blast with him. I think over the course of the year we solved all the world's problems—probably for the worse, but we solved them.

I remember playing a game in San Francisco last year. Someone hit a ball and I dove for it and caught it. Andy came running over to cover the base. My throw was a little high. He had to reach for it and as soon as it hit his glove he tripped. He held on to the ball, but he fell over the base. I started laughing so hard. Here's a forty-year-old man with receding hair, and to see him rolling around on the field in front of thirty thousand people at Candlestick Park just struck me as funny.

And he looked up at me and said, "Dammit, take it yourself. I'm too fuckin' old for this." And that's when I really lost it. I was trying not to laugh but when he said that I thought I was going to die. And we were losing the game, too.

I've said that pitchers are a breed apart, but Andy is different. He's pretty veteranish. Look at the guys he's played with: Nolan Ryan, Mike Scott. He's learned from them. He's been around. I mean, he's a one-pitch pitcher, and he's been doing it for years and years and years. You always know what he's going to throw. Guys on first, taking their lead, sometimes they look back at me and say, "Bet he throws his slider." And I say, "No shit. What else is he going to throw?"

To be around as long as he has throwing one pitch, that's amazing. But other guys can learn from that. A guy throws a 95-mile-an-hour fastball and he wants to throw something else in a tough spot? Give me a break. All Andy throws is the slider. Granted, now, it's the best slider in the world. But one great pitch can carry you a long way.

People see the funny things he does, like putting the fake hair on his head, or they hear about the funny things he says. But they don't see the competitiveness. It's the same thing with Lenny; people read about the gambling and the car wreck. With Andy they don't read about the preparation.

They read his Shallow Thoughts, like "Why do you drive on a parkway and park on a driveway?" I think my favorite one is "Why is there an expiration date on sour cream?" That's the one I always remember. I asked him about it once, and he looked at me, dead serious, and he said, "I still can't understand why." I think no one has ever given him an answer to that question, and it bothers him. Maybe he needs to call and ask the Food and Drug Administration.

And he promotes that image, because that's the way he is. He's fucked up. When he's out there pitching, he's dead serious. But when something funny happens, he laughs. He's been pitching long enough to know it's just a game. Like that play in San Francisco; he had two big strawberries on his knees. He was in the trainers' room after the game getting bandages put on so he wouldn't get blood on his pants. And he said it was the first time in fifteen years he'd had to do that. He was kind of proud, like it was a war wound.

All in all, we were quite a group. It's like someone said during the playoffs: "If the Braves were America's Team, we must have been America's Most Wanted."

People in West Virginia have cars. We have indoor plumbing. We use forks and spoons.

HERE'S SOMETHING I'LL BET A LOT OF people don't know: George Brett was born in West Virginia. Okay, so he left when he was a month old and he may have never been back, but he's going to the Hall of Fame and he's a West Virginian.

A lot of people seem to think it's funny that I live there.

When I played for the Padres, they used to get on me all the time. Garry Templeton and Ed Whitson started it. Now, Whitson is from Tennessee, and he's not from some metropolis, either. But they started calling me a dumb hillbilly and it stuck.

Then Tim Flannery jumped in. Every time somebody would ask him about me, he'd say, "He's just a dumb hillbilly. He don't know what's going on." Flannery is the one who started that story about me, the one where we're on the team bus in Chicago, driving past Lake Michigan, and I supposedly asked which ocean that was. That never happened. I knew it wasn't an ocean. I just didn't know what lake it was.

In the minors, one of my managers said I reminded him of an Alabama truck driver. That stuck for a while. Then it followed me into the big leagues where I became a dumb hillbilly.

Well, I live in the hills. But I don't think I'm that dumb. I'm getting dumber every year, but I don't think I've reached stupidity yet.

People in West Virginia have cars. We have indoor plumbing. We use forks and spoons. We don't have cable, but we do have satellite dishes. Sure, you're going to see some pickup trucks with gun racks on the back. You're going to see rebel flags, long hair, jeans—but that's the way everyone dresses back there, so it ain't no big deal.

Here's something else I'll bet a lot of people don't know: I was born in Charleston, West Virginia, on February 9, 1961, but my family moved when I was a year old—to New Jersey. Northern New Jersey, in fact, Bergen County, right outside New York City.

That's where I learned to play baseball, more or less. We played sports all the time. Where we live now, it would be hard because you might have neighbors close by, but they might not have kids. But where we lived in Jersey there was a family, the Ennis family, nearby that had two boys, Kevin and Mickey, one a year younger than me and one a year older. They played with me and my brothers—football, basketball, baseball, anything. What else did we know how to do? We went out and played ball.

We played stickball in the streets. There were some Little League fields, but we were at an age where our parents didn't want us to be three or four miles away all day, so we painted bases on the street and we played stickball. That's how we learned. I also went to games at Yankee Stadium. We were only fifteen or twenty minutes outside the city.

We lived there until I was ten or eleven years old. I think that's where I picked up a little of that New Jersey attitude.

Then we moved back to West Virginia. And I hated it. Everything was slowed down so much. I cried and argued and said I wanted to go back to New Jersey, because that was the only home I really knew. It wasn't until later, probably when I was in high school, that I started realizing what a good place West Virginia is to live. There's hardly any crime, and it's so laid-back. In New Jersey I learned to get excited about games, and in West Virginia I learned to calm down once they were over. The difference between the two places is like night and day.

I was the youngest of four brothers. Joe is the oldest; he's ten years older than I am. Tom is four years older and Larry is a year older. We had a normal childhood. We weren't rich and we weren't poor. Middle of the road.

Tom and Larry and I played Whiffle ball together. Joe played when he came home from college, but he was a lot bigger than we were: he went off to college when I was seven. The way we played, you had to hit the same way as each guy on the team you were supposed to be. Eddie Murray was my favorite player. I always pretended to be the Orioles because they were one of the closest teams to us and because they had Murray and Ken Singleton and Al Bumbry, so I could bat left-handed. I couldn't hit right-handed worth a damn; I tried it when I was pretending to be Brooks Robinson or Dan Baylor. But I always liked Eddie Murray. He never popped off, and he put up large numbers every year.

Joe is the ultimate shit talker. He can talk trash with the best of them. He told a fan in Atlanta during the playoffs to shut up, then added, "And tell your ugly fuckin' wife to shut up, too."

The four of us were home over Christmas this winter. Tom was telling us about being in the bathroom at Veterans Stadium during the playoffs. He was talking to another guy from Philadelphia, a fan. And the guy asks him who he is. He says, "I'm John Kruk's brother Tom." And the fan goes, "You can't be. You're nice. I've met his one brother and he's an asshole." About then Joe came walking by and said, "Yeah, here I am."

My dad worked in a bottle factory, fixing the big metal molds. His name is Frank, but everybody calls him Moe. I think he got that nickname back in high school and that's what everybody still calls him. Sometimes people come up to me and say they know my dad, Frank, and I don't say too much because I know they must not know him very well. Nobody calls him Frank.

My mom, Lena, also worked in the bottle factory. They both played sports. My mother played on a basketball team and they tell me she was pretty good. It seemed like the first thing we all did as kids was to pick up a ball. I didn't get to see Joe play too much; he went to a small college in North Carolina, a five-foot-nine-inch point guard who was a pretty good shooter. One night he scored, I think, thirty points in a game against Lloyd Free. Free didn't play much defense even then, but it's still good to be able to tell people that my brother scored thirty points against a guy who went on to play a lot of years in the NBA.

We had moved to New Jersey because my dad got transferred, and as soon as he had a chance, he got transferred back to West Virginia. I really didn't adapt too well at first. The only thing that made me happy was playing sports; that was all I seemed to have in common with anyone back there who was my age. Some of them would have to get up early and do chores. Some of them had to work to help their families make ends meet. When I woke up, if I wasn't going to school, I played ball.

I wasn't an angel or anything. One time I shot out a neighbor's car window with a BB gun. I just did normal stuff, though. Nothing really bad.

There was a guy who lived across the street—now, back there, across the street means across the street and through the neighbor's yard and then you cross over into a field. Well, across the way he had built a nine-hole golf course. That's the kind of courses we have in West Virginia because there are so many mountains it's hard to find enough flat land for eighteen holes.

Anyway, the people who were playing would hit their shots, and when I was fourteen or fifteen years old I'd run out onto the course and steal their golf balls. I did it for a long time until they finally caught me. They did the worst thing they could have done. I wish they had taken me to the police. I wish they had taken me to jail. But they did something much worse than that: they took me to my parents.

I was disciplined. Heavily. With a belt. Nowadays you can't hit kids, even your own. They can take you to court. But I took my beatings. I didn't like them, but I took them. You lock a kid in his room today and what's that? You're grounded. So they sit in there for a week and play Nintendo and listen to the CD player—same stuff they'd be doing anyway.

I think I appreciate what I have now because I realize what my parents went through. When we lived in New Jersey, I hardly ever saw my father. I was at that age where I was starting to play ball and I wanted to be around him, but he was never there. I really didn't understand until later, after we'd moved back, why he wasn't; it was because he had to work double shifts. He had to sacrifice that much just so his kids could play ball and get better in sports. And he did it because that's what his dad had done for him and his brothers. He'd get home at six o'clock in the morning, sleep until ten, and then he'd go out and referee a high school football game on a Saturday afternoon. Then he'd go right back to work.

A long time before that, before we moved to New Jersey, he used to referee high school basketball games. I always followed Jerry West in the pros because he was from West Virginia and my dad had worked some of his high school games. I remember my dad saying that he was so good in high school, so much better than anybody else, that he just got the shit beat out of him every night. If he was going in for a layup, they'd knock him into the wall. He'd just pick himself up, make the foul shots, and go back to the other end to play defense. He never said a word, never complained.

If our mother hadn't been so interested in sports, we might have gone different ways and done different things. But she encouraged us. Our parents never told us what to do, but once we decided what we wanted, they did whatever they could to get us where we had to be to play. And you know, when you have four boys and one is playing in a league in one part of town and another is playing in a different league somewhere else and your two youngest boys are playing in a third league, that's quite a sacrifice. But if my parents hadn't driven me to all those games, I wouldn't be where I am today.

They're one of the biggest reasons I was so happy to be traded from San Diego to Philadelphia. When I was out there, they were maybe able to come out every other year for a week or so. My mom doesn't like to fly, so they had to drive out. Now they can come up just about every weekend we're at home.

They don't work anymore, either. After the first good contract I signed, after two or three years in the big leagues, I talked them into retiring. It wasn't something they asked for or anything, but they had done so much for me, I felt the least I could do was help them out with whatever they needed. It was only right.

One more thing about my dad. He looks exactly like Don Zimmer, who managed the Red Sox, Padres, Rangers, and Cubs and now is a coach for the Colorado Rockies. Even before I started playing in the big leagues, people would comment on that. One time I was at home watching the 1975 World Series between the Red Sox and Reds. Zim was coaching third for Boston. A bunch of people were at the house watching the game and they were all saying, "Damn, he looks just like Moe."

The first time I ever met Zim, I said, "You look just like my dad. Identical." I always wanted to get a picture of them together, and last year I did. The next time I see Zim, I'm going to ask him to sign it for me.

When our family moved to Keyser, West Virginia, from New Jersey, everything was a lot less expensive, so my dad only had to work one shift. We saw him all the time, and we liked that a lot better.

After we moved back, he managed me for three years, and that worked out fine. The only thing I didn't like was that he wanted me to play shortstop. I didn't want to. The first day I made three errors. The thing was, he didn't like to move people around. When I pitched, my brother played shortstop, so when my brother pitched, my dad wanted me to play shortstop; otherwise, he'd have to move the guy who was playing third to shortstop and a guy from the outfield to play third and the guy from first to play outfield and I'd go to first, or something like that. So he thought it was just easier if I went to short. He told me there was nothing to it, that all I had to do was catch the ball and throw it to first. I said I guessed I could do that. Then I made three errors.

You know how it is when you're young. I had a temper and I threw my glove and I said, "I'm not playing that position ever again. Put me somewhere else." And he said that was fine. He said, "If you don't want to play where I tell you, then go the hell home. I don't want you on this team. If you don't play shortstop, you ain't playing."

In order to continue playing, I had to play shortstop. So that's what I did.

That made a big impression on me. I could sort of see how a guy in the big leagues could get into a confrontation with the manager. After all, the manager's a professional, but so is the player. But I go back and I see kids yelling at their coach. They don't have any respect for a guy who is giving up his time and working for free to try and help them. I don't understand that.

That situation with my father taught me to respect my coaches and the other men in charge. That was a pretty useful lesson, because when I got to the pros I was not a high draft pick, so I knew that in any given year in the minors, if I pissed off the manager, if I acted like an asshole, I might never play again. I realized that they're there and in charge for a reason, and if they tell you to do something, you'd damn well better do it.

Once my dad made it clear that I might never play again, I was more than happy to go to shortstop. Of course, I always wanted to pitch. When I went to Potomac State College in Keyser, I was a good hitter, but I still thought pitching was more fun. That was before I saw how much those pitchers ran.

In high school we played right after school. We didn't take batting practice or anything, we just kind of went out and loosened up and then we pitched. Then the game was over and we went home. But when I got to Potomac State, I saw the pitchers running and running and running. Plus they had to put ice on their arms and they were doing all these exercises.

And I said, "I think I'm an outfielder."

The coach there was named Jack Reynolds. He was real good, real smart. He didn't put up with nothing. So I played for my dad in the summer and he didn't put up with nothing. Then I played for Coach Reynolds, and he didn't put up with nothing.

It all prepared me to play for Larry Bowa.

Jack Reynolds had his own way of doing things. Before you touched a ball, you had to run. Left field was probably 280 feet from the plate, but it went up a hill. There was a practice football field up there, so we had to run around the regular football field then up the hill to the other football field and around that and then back to the dugout. We had to do that twice before we touched a bat or a ball. If you touched a ball or a bat first, you had to run four times. That helped me learn that I'd better listen, I'd better not stray or I'm not going to make it. I damn sure didn't want to run four of those laps.

Actually, I had gone to junior college on a basketball scholarship. I dropped football when I was in eighth grade. The game wasn't too much fun. I mean, I liked it. I just didn't enjoy the headaches.

Basketball was my sport in high school. I just played baseball so I could play basketball. The thing was, back then, if you played basketball they wanted you to run track in the spring, I guess to keep you in shape or something. That didn't make much sense to me. I mean, track season ends and then you have all summer and all fall before basketball starts again. So what difference does it make?

So I went out for track. I didn't know what I was doing. They said to run a mile or so. I ran the mile. I ran it one day in practice and I never went back. I knew right away that wasn't for me. So I started playing baseball instead, but it was really just something I did to keep from having to run track.

I was a pretty good student in high school. I made B's. In college, though, I was real bad. I was there for one reason, to play ball. That isn't the right reason. I know that. I should have studied, but I didn't want to. I couldn't picture myself going through four years of college. That's not the right way to go for everyone, though; I just got lucky.

I don't even remember if I had a major. It didn't matter. I was gone from seven-thirty every morning until nine or ten every night. I'd practice basketball, and then the baseball team would come into the gym and start running and hitting in the cage and doing all the drills.

But things didn't work out between me and the college basketball coach. He still lives in town; I see him occasionally, and it's all forgotten now, but the problem was he was forced to take the job. He really didn't want to coach basketball, really didn't care about it. It was like, "Here's the ball. Go play." A couple times he didn't even show up for practice, so half the players wouldn't show up either. There was no discipline. I wasn't used to that. I was used to having a coach who said, "It's this way or the highway." But that didn't happen in college, and I just said the heck with it, I wasn't going to play basketball anymore. I went down and talked to the baseball coach, and thank God I did. I was doing good in basketball, but let's face it, I wasn't going to have a career in that sport. I was too short. Too slow. Too white.

I started devoting full time to baseball and I really started enjoying it. But after the 1980–1981 school year Potomac State dropped baseball so I had to transfer about twenty miles away to Allegany Community College.

I wanted to go to West Virginia University. I think every kid who grows up in the state dreams about going there. There was another guy on our team, Jeff Reynolds, who was drafted by the Yankees and played a few years in their organization. We both wanted to go to the U., but the coach there said we had both reached our peak and weren't going to get any better.

I think he was just pissed off because we used to play them every fall and we pummeled them. Their baseball program wasn't real good. We punished them, and maybe that was why he wouldn't take us. I really resented it for a long time. If West Virginia's football team played in a bowl game, everybody in the state was rooting for the Mountaineers—everybody but me. I wanted them to lose all their games. I realize now that's childish, but I was really pissed off that I was only eighteen years old and here's a guy telling me I'd already reached my peak.

I guess I'm finally over it, though, because I root for them now. I wanted them to beat Florida in the Sugar Bowl, but that's just recently. When Major Harris was their quarterback a couple of years ago and they played Notre Dame for the national championship, I didn't want them to win.

Back when I was in school, I wasn't really thinking about playing professional baseball. I'd never seen a scout. I didn't know who they were, and I didn't think they knew where West Virginia was.

But we had a guy on the team named Holly Martin. All the scouts came to watch him. Then Jeff Reynolds was drafted and signed. I thought, "Man, he got drafted. He's going to play pro ball." That's when I really started working on my game. It was the first time I'd really worked at anything.

My big break came in the summer of 1981. I was playing in Virginia, for New Market in the Shenandoah Valley League. I was only there a couple of weeks. Tom Browning, who went on to play with the Reds, was on my team. We played against Bob Patterson, who has pitched with several teams in the majors. That June I was drafted by the Padres in the third round of the secondary phase. At the time, I wasn't even sure where San Diego was.

Tom Browning got drafted, too, and we went in to tell the coach we were leaving. He said, "You're making a big mistake, you'll never make it. You'd better stay here." Tom Browning was our best pitcher, and I was leading the team in hitting. So we signed, and we both made it. It's funny. Browning and I were talking about that last year. But neither one of us could remember that coach's name.

I was ready to get away by then, but I always look forward to getting back to West Virginia now. Some people think it's like you're living next door to Jed Clampett before he was shootin' at some food and up through the ground came the bubblin' crude. But that doesn't bother me.

Sometimes it works to my advantage. Some days I don't feel like talking, so I just act dumber than hell and people leave me alone. Life is slower back there. There's not the traffic and the hustle like there is in a big city. I couldn't live in a city. I hate walking out of someplace you live and all you see are cars and people. If I want to go outside my house and pee off the front porch, I can do that. No one can see me and that's the way I like it. I have privacy.

I don't think we ever lock the doors. Nobody comes up where we live. If somebody does come up and wants to borrow a chain saw or something and we're not there, they take it. They'll bring it back. Or if I see them before they're through with it, they'll tell me they have it.

When I was a kid, we had a pretty big backyard. We made a baseball field out of it. And maybe we'd decide that everybody would come over at nine o'clock in the morning and we'd play baseball, play all day. It was nothing to get up at a quarter to nine and find a couple guys in the kitchen making sandwiches. That's the way it is in West Virginia. You want a drink, you go into somebody's house. You don't have to ask.

If you tried that in Philadelphia, they'd shoot you.

Where my parents live, they've got cable and city water. They're talking about putting cable out where I live, and I hope they do. The satellite dish goes out sometimes when it storms.

And I've got to have television. I'd rather have that than any-thing else in the house.

I don't hunt much anymore. One day last winter, though, a few of us were sitting in the hot tub when I looked out the window and saw a deer. It was real cold outside. I didn't tell anybody. I just got out and got my rifle. I put on my work boots. I was standing there in my bathing suit and boots and I was starting to get icicles on me. I dropped it with one shot and then jumped back into the hot tub. Later we cleaned it and ate it. Some people think that's cruel, but venison is good meat. And the deer are going to die anyway; so many of them starve to death when it snows.

Another nice thing about being from West Virginia is that there are so few of us that we're almost like a fraternity. Don Robinson was a veteran when I first came into the league and we didn't play on the same team, but he was always nice to me because I was from West Virginia.

One time I hit a home run off him. I was just a young guy and I'm sitting in the clubhouse after the game. The clubhouse man came and told me there was a call for me. I picked up the phone and it was Robby. He's cussing me up one side and down the other. And I'm thinking, you know, Is this what it's like when you hit a home run in the big leagues? Then he says, "You should have hit that pitch, it was a horseshit pitch. I would have been really mad at you if you hadn't hit it out."

Another good friend of mine is Leo Mazzone, the pitching coach for the Braves. He lives in Maryland now, but he was born and grew up just across the river in West Virginia. He had pitched in a summer league, and he did a clinic when I was in junior college. Eventually we started talking and found out we were a lot alike. We sometimes barbecue together at two-thirty in the morning in the middle of the winter, or we sit around and watch basketball together. We have a good time.

Another thing I like to do when I'm home is go down to the

car wash my friend, Steve Taylor, runs. I just enjoy hanging out, talking to whoever comes in.

You know, there are so many guys from California and Florida, states like that, playing in the big leagues. In a state like West Virginia, it isn't as easy to learn to play because there are so many mountains. There's not as much clear room for good fields, and you can't play year-round because of the weather.

Still, where I was from, there were some good athletes who were just never seen by scouts. Or they enjoyed being farmers and they really didn't want to leave. I was lucky because there were two other excellent players on my junior college team and the scouts heard about them and came to see them, so they saw me, too.

George Brett didn't have that problem, by the way. His family moved to California.

I'll still take West Virginia.

One of the reasons I like playing first base is that there's somebody to talk to during the game. It can get lonely in the outfield.

TOP OF THE FIRST INNING. SECOND GAME

of the playoffs. We had won the first game and Veterans Stadium was electric. The Braves had Otis Nixon on third with two outs.

And Fred McGriff, Atlanta's first baseman, crushed Tommy Greene's first pitch. Hit it into the upper deck in right field.

In the bottom of the first inning, I walked. We had runners on first and second with one out. We're trying to come back against Greg Maddux. All he's doing is winning his second straight Cy Young Award. So naturally I'm still thinking about McGriff's home run.

I mean, call it professional respect or whatever. When a guy hits a home run like that, even if it's against you, you have to respect that.

So I asked him, "Did you break your bat on that one?"

Now, he's one of the nicest guys around. But he's real quiet. He usually doesn't say a whole lot. He's probably too quiet.

He looked at me real seriously. He said, "No, I think I hit that one pretty good."

I said, "No shit. I figured that out when I noticed those people falling out of the upper deck. I think you killed a family of four with that bomb."

Then he caught on and started laughing.

I like talking to players on the other team during the game. It takes my mind off different things, helps get rid of the nervous energy. It relaxes me just to b.s. with those guys. I mean, I like my teammates, but I see them all the time. It's nice to see somebody else from time to time.

One of the reasons I like playing first base is that there's somebody to talk to during the game. It can get lonely in the outfield.

Sometimes I don't like it so much, though. We had a game against the Cardinals at Busch Stadium last year where they had eighteen base runners in the first three innings and scored fourteen runs. It was like Meet the Cardinals Day down at first base. I didn't care for that much. Same for a couple of those games in the World Series; I enjoyed talking to the Blue Jays, but at times it got ridiculous.

I've had some pretty good conversations out there. One of my favorites is Tommy Sandt, the first base coach for the Pirates. Every time I go out there, he's got a new joke for me. Sometimes if we're way ahead or way behind, I almost can't wait for us to make three outs so I can go back out there and hear another joke. Tommy's got some good ones.

The amazing thing is, he never repeats himself. We play the Pirates four series a year, usually three games in a series. That's over a hundred jokes and he never tells the same one twice. I don't know how he does it.

I enjoy talking to runners when they get to first base. Marquis Grissom, I talk to him a lot when we play Montreal. One of the reasons is that he's on base so much. One game last year, we were playing the Expos, and Larry Walker got on first. He started telling me I should get a haircut, all that shit. He started running his fingers through my hair. I told him he'd better quit or people might start looking at us funny.

You can talk to catchers when you're at bat, too. I talk to Joe Oliver all the time when we play Cincinnati. One time, Tim Belcher was pitching for them. He was shutting us out. Mitch Williams came in late in the game. He threw a pitch behind one guy, then hit the next guy.

I was leading off the next inning. I figured I was going to get drilled. I said, "Well, Joe, where's he going to hit me?"

He just laughed. I didn't get hit, though. Maybe that's just because I'm so nimble and quick.

Another time, Rob Dibble came in to pitch for the Reds. He was real wild that night, but thank God most of the pitches he was throwing to me were wild to the outside. Oliver said, "Hope you don't have any right-handed batters coming up."

Dibble ended up getting out of the inning.

One time I was up to bat—I think it was against the Mets —and here comes the pitch and it's right at my waist. I don't know how it kept from hitting me in the stomach.

I said, "Hell, I must be losing weight. That's the only way I don't get hit by that pitch."

And the catcher—it might have been Charlie O'Brien—said, "That's our book on you. Pitch under your belt where you can't see it."

Another time I took a pitch right down the middle. I mean, a perfect strike. And the umpire called it a ball. The catcher started bitching. After he got through, I stepped back in, looked down and said, "I guess that one must have caught a little too much of the plate."

Sometimes it still seems amazing to me that I get to talk to some of these guys, that I can just talk to them and they'll talk back to me.

Like Dale Murphy. Besides going to the World Series, playing with him was probably the highlight of my career. You know, you never heard anybody say anything bad about him. Never. When he was on the other team I thought, Well, we only play him twelve times a year; even I could be nice twelve times a year. You just think to yourself that he can't really be that nice all the time. You figure you just caught him on his good days.

And then he comes over to your team and you realize he's just everything you could have imagined and more. Even then, I don't think any of us completely realized how lucky we were to play with someone like that until we went back to Atlanta and they had a night for him. They showed highlights of his career up on the video screen. And we saw a World Series MVP, our pitching coach Johnny Podres, bawling while he watched them. That tells you what a class person Murf is. I'll never meet another guy like that. Never. He's even better than he was billed to be.

Tony Gwynn helped me get my first glove contract. We had known each other in the minors. He got to the big leagues before I did, though. One day he was talking to the rep from Rawlings. Gwynn said, "You should take care of him." So the guy started sending me gloves every year.

Still haven't figured out how to use 'em, but I've got 'em.

Roger McDowell is always a treat to be around. He's like a kid who played Little League, joked around and had fun, and he just kept it going. He's an intelligent man, but in baseball terms, he's a ten-year-old. That's just the way he approaches the game. One day we were in Chicago in April, and it was snowing. We were in a snow delay, so he went out on the field wearing football gear, having guys throw passes to him. Then he went out and had the bleacher bums throw passes to him.

You know, Roger's one of the few visiting players that the bleacher bums look forward to having come to town. They like him. He entertains them. Me, I'm glad I play in the infield now so I don't have to go out there and listen to them. They just abuse me, so I don't even go out there for batting practice.

But Roger has them eating out of the palm of his hand. And he's just as funny with everybody. It's like he goes home in the winter, and while some guys play golf and some guys just relax, he goes home and works on his jokes. Practices them. He must, because he has the hotfoot down to an art. He probably went out to some field and sat in a dugout and put a hotfoot on himself, lit it, and ran out onto the field to see how long it took. He must have, because when he puts one on the first base coach or the third base coach during the season, it flares at just the right time.

You never know what's going to happen when he's around. Somebody called me after last season and asked me if I wanted to play in the MTV Rock and Jock game. I asked who all was going to be there. She said, "Well, Roger, of course." And I said, "That's good enough for me. You don't have to tell me any more. I'll be there."

I've never seen anybody quite like Dennis Cook. He's a pitcher from Texas we got from the Giants in the trade that also brought Terry Mulholland and Charlie Hayes.

Dennis was different. He's the only guy I've ever seen that

Lenny Dykstra would call down to our end of the locker room just because he liked to listen to him talk. He made Lenny laugh, and he would just sit there listening to Cookie's stories. If I'm telling Lenny a story, or if anybody else is, he's liable to just get up in the middle of the story and walk away. But he loved listening to the Cookie talk.

Some guys, when they're in the minor leagues, they dream about getting to the major leagues. They think, I might get a glove contract. I might get a shoe contract. You get that and you're the happiest man in the world. All Cookie wanted was a Wranglers contract. I mean, he didn't care if he had spikes or a glove as long as he had those Wranglers. He wore his boots everywhere. He was chewing some gum once and dropped it in the dugout, right in some tobacco spit or whatever, and put it right back in his mouth.

He thought he was a hitter. If he hit a grounder to the infield, he'd dive into first base headfirst. They had to tell him not to do that.

Cookie threw up behind the mound once. It was in Philly. He stepped off the mound and reached down like he was picking up the resin bag, but he puked instead. Then he went right back to pitching. He always said he wanted to make enough money playing baseball so he could buy a goat farm. Like I said, he was a little different.

I've always liked talking to Randy Ready, whether we were on the same team or he was playing for somebody else. But it's hard sometimes. He has a different vocabulary than anybody else I know. If we went out together someplace in San Diego, he'd sit there talking with his surfer friends, and it was like I was in a foreign country. I never did quite grasp all that surfer lingo.

One time he was playing second base. Somebody hit a pop-up real high. He's standing there waiting for the ball to come down, and he's yelling, "Down elevator! Fourth floor, Sporting

Goods! Third Floor, Housewares!" I guess that was his way of saying he was going to take it.

Anything guys do together is going to make the team closer. The Phillies have a team golf tournament during spring training every year. It's a lot of fun, but some guys take it seriously, too. They want to win.

When I was in San Diego, we had a golf tournament of our own. Tim Stoddard ran it. It was called the Tim Stoddard Fucked Up Open. It was played on a little par-three course. They had lights, so we started at midnight. There were all kinds of rules. Like, if you hit the ball on the green, you had to take a drink of this. If you didn't hit the ball on the green, you had to take two drinks of something else.

You see how the tournament got its name.

I was in a cart with Goose Gossage. I was a rookie, in my first spring training camp, so I don't know how I got paired with him. But there we were, driving over this hill. I was driving one way. Goose said, "No, no, my ball is over the other way." So I jerked the cart around and he rolled out of the cart and down the hill.

I thought, "Oh, man, here's a guy who's probably going to the Hall of Fame. I ain't played a day in the big leagues. And now I'll never play in the big leagues because I just dumped Goose Gossage down that hill."

I think he hurt his knee, but he never told the team what really happened. He kind of told them he got hurt doing something else.

That was back in the days when I didn't say too much, especially to the older players. I've gotten over that by now.

Even if you'd been on a bus for sixteen hours and were stiff and hungry and didn't feel worth a damn, you had to go out and play well.

IT SEEMS KIND OF FUNNY TO ME NOW TO

see players who are drafted and then hold out for a big signing bonus. The Padres told me they'd give me $2,500 to sign, and I didn't argue; I was happy to have the money and I was on my way to Walla Walla, Washington, in the Class A Northwest League.

There wasn't much to do in Walla Walla. The road trips weren't any better: Bend, Eugene, Medford. I didn't adapt any better than I did when my family moved from New Jersey back to West Virginia. It was the first time I'd really been away from home, and I was only making about $500 a month. That didn't go far, even in 1981 in Walla Walla, Washington.

I thought I was pretty lucky when another guy on the team and I found a room to rent from a family in town. That's the way most players at that level get by. The family seemed real nice, and we moved into a room in the basement.

What we didn't realize was that they ran a day-care center upstairs. We realized it real quick the next morning at eight o'clock when all the kids started screaming. I think that's when I decided I probably didn't want children.

I only batted .242 that year, but I had some fun. Walla Walla is where I first met Tony Gwynn, who was drafted the same time I was. It was another situation where two guys who didn't seem to have much in common—a black guy from San Diego State and a white guy from Allegany Community College—ended up becoming good friends.

Tony had a pretty good sense of humor. We usually ate together, so one day in Medford I asked him if he wanted to get some lunch. He said that he had some things to do and that he would catch me later. A little later I went out to a restaurant, and I was stopped by a policeman. He asked me if I knew Tony Gwynn. I said I did. He said I had to come with him to the jailhouse, that Tony had been arrested. I said, "No, that can't be true. There must be some mistake. Tony is the nicest guy in the world."

We went to get in the cruiser and Tony was in there, laughing. The policeman was a friend of his, and we spent the rest of the day driving around with him. I think we were looking for a guy who had been accused of shooting somebody.

You could tell even then that Tony could hit. He batted

.331, which led the league, and was moved up to Amarillo before the season was over and made it to the big leagues the next year. I finished the year in Walla Walla, but I guess I had shown them enough to be moved up to Reno, another Class A team in the California League, for the 1982 season.

There was some beautiful country around there and, of course, legalized gambling. I didn't gamble much, at least partly because I was making just $700 a month. But on off days, we'd walk in the hills around the lake. Sometimes you'd see women sunbathing topless. Sometimes you'd see people doing the deed.

I started to feel more comfortable that year and one reason was that I had the perfect roommate. I roomed with Kevin McReynolds. I was shy around strangers, but he wouldn't say a word to *anybody*. That helped me break out and become a little more outgoing. If we went to the grocery store and he couldn't find what he was looking for, he wouldn't ask; he'd have me ask for him. I had to do it because he was bigger than me. And that's how I learned to talk to people.

I had no choice. Man, he was huge back then. But he could play. He'd been the Padres first-round draft choice the year before, but he couldn't play because he had a bad knee. But he came right into Reno and batted .376 before he got moved up. We had a great time. We were just like brothers; we'd get along great for a few days and then we'd fight. I lost most of the fights.

Life in the low minors means long bus trips. It means crawling off a bus with no money. You go play and you've gotta love it—at least, that's what they tell you. Even if you'd been on a bus for sixteen hours and were stiff and hungry and didn't feel worth a damn, you had to go out and play well, because if you didn't you weren't going to move up.

In 1983 I was promoted to Double-A Beaumont in the Texas League. The Beaumont Golden Gators. That was the most fun I had playing baseball up to that point. The players were so close. We had a blast. On off days we'd have pool parties; we all lived in the same apartment complex, and if we had a day off they'd close the pool to everybody but the players and their girlfriends. Of course, you know how enthusiastic young ballplayers can get. I don't think anyone would have wanted to be down there with us.

Then we'd go to the ballpark and we'd destroy people. We just won so much. We won the championship.

I had my best roommate ever in Beaumont—Steve Garcia. He's from northern California and I'm from West Virginia, so that makes us opposites right there. But we were so much alike. For example, he liked to turn the air conditioning on full blast at night and keep the room freezing cold while we slept. So did I. We did everything together. I mean, everything. Even today, whenever we go to San Francisco, we get together.

But that year was also an awakening. We won and we were all close and we had a great time, and we thought that was the way it was going to be; we'd all go to Triple-A the next year and we'd win there, then someday we'd all be with the Padres and we'd win in San Diego, too.

But it didn't happen that way. We won and that was it. I was one of the few guys from that team who went to Triple-A the next year. The rest of them were sent back or released.

Steve Garcia was a second baseman who stole a lot of bases and hit .300 every year. He didn't go up. We had another guy, Mark Gillespie, who hit .333 or something with more than 30 home runs and 130 runs batted in. He was named Most Valuable Player of the league. And the next year they sent him back to Double-A—as the fourth outfielder. Unbelievable.

That showed me that baseball wasn't just a game anymore. You know, maybe you'd talk to some guys who were in the big leagues, and they were always talking about how you have to play for yourself, but it doesn't sink in because you're so used to playing team baseball. But then you see things like that, and it makes you stop and think. You have to realize in the minors that while you want to win as a team, the big club is looking at you as individuals. When you get up to the majors it's a team game again, but on the way there it's what you do for yourself that matters.

And even then, like with Mark Gillespie, you just can't figure out *what* they're looking for. I thought, Man, if they can send *him* back, what the hell is going to happen to everyone else? We had great players. You always hear guys saying that there are other organizations, that if you play well there are scouts from all the other teams watching, and if another team likes you they'll get you somehow. But I always thought that since I was drafted by the Padres, I was going to play for the Padres if I made it that far. I never thought about playing for another team. It kind of makes you bitter toward the whole situation when your friends don't get a chance.

You get to a point where you wonder if anything will ever be good enough. You see what happens with someone like Mark Gillespie: they sent him back and he was never the same again. There is no doubt in my mind he could be playing in the big leagues right now if they gave him the opportunity. They said he didn't have a position, but I've seen a lot of outfielders in the big leagues worse than he was. He was a switch-hitter and, damn, he could hit. What power. There was only one home run hit in our ballpark in the first half of the season, and that was by a visiting player. And Gillespie still hit thirty-three home runs that season.

So everybody just sat there wondering what kind of year you have to have to get to the big leagues. It's so different now. A guy has a decent year at Double-A and all of a sudden he's a can't-miss prospect and then he's in the big leagues. Then he plays two or three years before people realize he really can't play. I'll tell you, there are guys in the big leagues right now who couldn't have played on that Double-A team.

We had some great times during that year in Texas. It was the first year Beaumont was in the league and we were winning, so people treated us like royalty.

One problem was that the team had been in Amarillo the year before, and when they moved the team to Beaumont they left us in the Western Division. Beaumont's, like, twenty-five miles from Louisiana, so that wasn't too smart. We had some monster bus trips in our own division to cities like El Paso and Midland and San Antonio. El Paso's only about seven hundred miles from Beaumont. And Little Rock—that trip to Little Rock took forever, too.

You could also get some pretty good weather in that part of the country. We had a tornado that blew the outfield fence down. I was in Mark Gillespie's apartment and I didn't know what the hell was going on. There was shit flying everywhere. His wife got into the bathtub and pulled a mattress over her head. Mark and I just sat there while the tornado blew all the windows out. I thought we were going to die. And hail—man, there were hailstones as big as golf balls. We were sitting there and all of a sudden the sliding glass door just started pushing in, so we went over and sat in the corner. That storm ripped the place up pretty good. At least we got a couple days off, with the outfield fence down and a couple light poles down, too. There was some serious damage.

Other times the weather was just an inconvenience. It seemed like every night it would rain right in the middle of batting practice. And the bugs were enormous. But we won so many games that it really didn't matter.

Every once in a while, you'd see something that could only happen in the minors. We had a pitcher early in the year who wasn't pitching too good and the organization decided to release him. They told him right before batting practice. He went to a bar close to the stadium, got drunk, and then he came back to the game. He sat right above the third base dugout and yelled at our manager the whole game. We all just stared at him.

Now that's a man who didn't take it too well.

I batted .341 and that was good enough to get me to Triple-A in Las Vegas the next year. It seemed that if you were consistent and put out good numbers every year, you didn't get a chance; you had to have that one outstanding year to even have a chance to move up to the next level, much less get to big league camp. When you see guys have great years and then keep getting sent back, it makes you sick to your stomach.

I really think minor leaguers today are too pampered. I played five full seasons in the minors. Now you have a guy who plays three years and doesn't put up nearly the kind of numbers I did, and he's bitching because he hasn't been called up yet. But it takes time to really learn the whole game.

Another thing I did to get more experience back in those days was to play winter baseball.

The Padres had just about all their top prospects play winter ball in Puerto Rico or the Dominican Republic or Venezuela. That's probably why I played in Mexico for five years.

I went down there the first time in 1983, after we finished our season at Beaumont, and I kind of liked it, so I kept going back. I played for Mexicali every one of those seasons. It was a border town, but I didn't realize that the first year. I could have lived in the United States and just crossed over for the games, but I didn't know that, so I lived in Mexico and that was something. In the major leagues we travel and we stay in the nicest hotels. You can call room service and they'll bring you anything you want. They have the best facilities you could dream about. When you've had the experience that I had in Mexico, you're always going to appreciate that.

I shared a hotel room with another guy. There was no restaurant. It was seriously hot, but the air conditioner didn't work, so we opened the windows. Well, we woke up in the middle of the night and there were pigeons flying all around the room. We had fallen asleep with the television on and they were attracted to the light, I guess. But it was the best hotel in town. Come to think of it, it was the only hotel in town.

I may not be the smartest guy in the world, but the next year I figured out that it would be better to live in California. Then the following year the owner liked me so much that he rented me a place right on a golf course. The team was very good to me. Every day I played golf and then I went to the ballpark.

They knew that I had played a lot of games in the summer, so they gave me some breaks the other players didn't get. If I felt like taking batting practice, I did; if I didn't feel like it, I didn't go. And none of the other players resented it, because players in that league don't get paid very much, but they make bonus money in the playoffs where they can double, triple, or even quadruple their salary.

One day some of the Mexican players were grumbling a little about my schedule. "He shows up when he wants. Why can't we? Why do we have to be here for all this when he doesn't?" That sort of thing. I couldn't answer because I didn't know much Spanish at the time, but one of the players, Houston Jiminez, a shortstop who used to play for the Twins, stood up. And he said, "When we get to the playoffs and this guy carries us through the playoffs and all that extra money starts coming in, then you'll understand why."

So then they all said, "Okay. We'll let him go."

That wasn't the only break I got. They had a lot of long bus trips. From Mexicali to Mazatlán was about twenty-four hours. Not only that, but they made you stop and get off the bus at check stations along the way. They'd get all the luggage out, empty everything out, hassle the Americans, and then put you back on the bus. It's three in the morning, they take all of your clothes out of your suitcase and then you have to put them all back in. It wasn't a whole lot of fun. And you'd have to do it at least twice during the trip. (Maybe that's why I don't bitch like some guys when we have to go through customs to get into and out of Canada.)

But they let the American guys fly. We'd drive to Tijuana, about an hour, and then fly to Mazatlán. The team told us to tell the other players that we were paying for our own flights. I ended up paying, but not for my own ticket. The first time I tried flying, it didn't go too smoothly; they stopped us at the airport and I didn't have working papers or a passport or a visa or anything, so they really hassled me. They put me in a room, strip-searched me and everything. So the next time I got one of the native guys to go with me. I said, "You're going with me. I'm paying for your flight. You're going to be my translator." He said, "You mean I don't have to ride that bus for twenty-four hours?" And it went better after that.

As I said, they let me do pretty much what I wanted. If we had clinched our division before the final trip of the year, which was always to Mazatlán, I didn't have to go. Every day they'd ask me if I was tired, because they didn't want me to be too tired for the playoffs. And every day I told them I wanted to play. But as soon as we clinched, they'd say, "You've got three days. Don't even show up." So I'd go to the beach and have some shrimp cocktails and a couple of beers. Then I'd walk back to the hotel and the other guys would be getting on a bus ready to go play a game—and they would all wave. They'd ask me if I'd be around later to go have a drink. There was no animosity. I got spoiled down there.

If I tried something like that now, I don't think it would go over too big.

Playing in Mexico was a great experience. The people were great. The fans knew all the players. You'd go to somebody's

house, and there would be dirt floors and wooden crates to sit
on, but they'd cook the most hellacious meal you've ever seen
—steaks and chicken and all this stuff. We'd sit around and
talk and eat and drink beer. You'd volunteer to go out and buy
more beer and they wouldn't let you; they were proud and they
wouldn't take your money, because they had invited you. You
were their guest. I'd sit there and I didn't know what they were
saying, but sooner or later we'd all be laughing.

I drank tequila down there. I'd never had it before, but some
places we went that's all there was, so I had no choice. I didn't
take it straight. I'd drink tequila and 7UP. Poppers. Sometimes
I'd drink it with ginger ale. Jeez. I blacked out one day. I woke
up on the beach and didn't really remember how I'd gotten
there. I figured out that maybe I shouldn't be drinking those.
But it was fun. I wouldn't trade those years for anything in the
world.

Of course, there were some really strange times, too.

Scary times. One time a guy on our team who was married
to a woman down there was standing around after the game,
holding his kid. He's standing there with his wife and we're
getting on the bus to go back to the hotel, and all of a sudden
he just threw the kid and took off screaming. His wife caught
the kid and he's running with a bat in his hand, chasing after
some guys.

I took off after him. I didn't know what the hell he was
doing. I found out later that during the game, while he was
warming up in the bullpen, some guys had thrown a bottle at
him from the stands. Now he saw these guys and he's chasing
them and yelling and cursing in Spanish.

I caught up to him and grabbed him. And the next thing I
know, there's a gun, some kind of rifle, in my face. A cop was
standing there holding this gun on me. He said something in
Spanish that I didn't understand. I just smiled and nodded all
the way back to the bus. My teammate didn't like it; he wanted
to go back after the guys, but I told him that if he did he was

on his own. I told him I wasn't getting shot just because he was pissed off at someone. And he got on the bus.

Not knowing Spanish could be a problem. No one told me the first year that the Mexican teams had what they consider spring training for winter ball. It starts about three weeks before the season. I didn't know that, so I just showed up when I was told, in time for the training period. None of the other Americans, the older guys who had been there before, showed up; they knew they didn't have to be there that early. I was kind of there by myself.

There was one guy down there, I think he went to school with Fernando Valenzuela. He had played some in the United States and knew pretty good English, but I didn't realize that until the fourth or fifth day of practice because he didn't say a word to me until then.

There was another guy who never said anything to me, either. He had this big Afro. He was walking past me one day and I just sort of said, "Jeez, look at that Afro."

He said, "Kiss my ass, fat boy."

I turned around. "You speak English?"

"Yep."

"Well, why the fuck didn't you speak to me? Nobody speaks to me. I'm here by myself. I don't know what the hell I'm doing. Why didn't you say something?"

"Testing you. I didn't know you."

After that we became good friends and played together every year I went down there. Then Houston Jiminez came in. And I wised up. After that I didn't go through that spring training. I just came in the day before the season started.

Getting something to eat was a problem. I'd just go to the restaurant and point to what I wanted on the menu: taco. I knew what a taco was. Here's how it went: I'd go over to this guy and I'd say, "Taco." And he'd give me one. Then I'd say, "Taco." And he'd give me another one.

I ate a lot of tacos.

Then I started learning a little bit of Spanish. I got to the point where I could go out and order food. Now if I need to ask somebody something in Spanish, I can get my point across. But I think going through that has helped me understand what some of the young Latin American players go through when they first sign in the States.

A lot of teams have the perception that the Latin players are lazy. But, I mean, when I was in Mexico they must have thought I was lazy, too, because they never saw me; the only time they saw me was at the ballpark. I was afraid to go anywhere else because I didn't know how to speak the language. And I was in my twenties, while most of those guys are sixteen or seventeen years old when they first sign. Organizations just stick them in a foreign country where they don't know the language.

I think it's getting better now. I think teams try to help them adjust. But I remember when I was in Reno and we had Ozzie Guillen on our team. He was the only Latin guy on the team. I felt bad for him, so I tried to help him as best I could. I tried to help him find a place to live. He knew a little English, but not enough to say, "I want a one-bedroom apartment." We taught him a little English, but you know how that goes—the first words he learned were the curse words.

The next year, in Beaumont, Ozzie lived right across from me and Steve Garcia. He'd started to pick up some English, but his wife came in and she didn't know a word. They didn't have a television, so when we went on the road, we'd give her the key to our apartment so she could at least come over and watch television.

You have to feel bad, really, when you hear people talking about them being lazy. Look at Mariano Duncan on our team. He finished third in the Rookie of the Year voting for the Dodgers in 1985. He was a skinny little shortstop back then. Look at him now—he's *strong*. He can drive a ball. He got that way by working hard, not by being lazy.

The fans are different in the winter leagues. One time before a game, we were running in the outfield. There was an old lady, she must have been mentally disturbed, because she walked out into the middle of the outfield and pulled up her dress and she peed right there on the field.

Security took care of it, though. Somebody came along and escorted her back to her seat. You just know that if that happened in the major leagues they would have tackled her and taken her back up the tunnel somewhere and beaten the hell out of her before they threw her in jail.

You also get a lot of stuff thrown at you. That more or less prepared me for Philadelphia.

Just kidding. In Philly they don't throw much at you. They're vocal, though; they boo you. But down there, the three worst things you can be are a visiting player, an American, and doing well. That's the Triple Crown. And when you have that going for you, you're going to get lemons and oranges thrown at you. And bottles. They drink the tequila and then throw the bottle at you. And then there are the guns and rifles.

See, they gamble a lot on the games down there. We played in one championship series where they had to have armed police in both stadiums. There had been some threats. A couple years later we were playing Mazatlán in the finals. There were a lot of guys who played in the majors on both teams, guys like Willie Aikens and Ron Jones and Eddie Miller and a bunch of others. A couple of us went out to eat dinner after Mexicali had won to take a lead in the series.

We were sitting in a restaurant. I had my back to another table that was real close, and all of a sudden this guy behind me leaned over and stuck something sharp in my ribs. And he told me, in real good English, that if I played the next day he was going to kill me. Then he turned around and stood up and walked out.

I didn't know what to do. I told one of the guys who was eating with us, a guy who had played down there forever, what had happened—that somebody had threatened me and stuck something in my side, and that I didn't know if it was the barrel of a gun, but I knew for a fact it wasn't his finger. I asked him what I should do.

He said, "Come on, let's go. We've got to get you back to the hotel." We went back to the hotel and we found the manager and the trainer. I told them what happened. They took me to a different hotel and got two policemen to stand outside my door. I couldn't leave the room. If I wanted something to eat, the policemen went and got me food.

They escorted me to the ballpark. They wouldn't let me take batting practice. They wouldn't let me play in the field. I was the designated hitter. I didn't run the bases. If I got on base they put someone in to run for me. I couldn't even sit in the dugout. After my at bats I hauled ass into the dugout and up the tunnel with the police and just sat there until it was my turn to bat again.

I have to admit, I didn't hit too good that day. I was kind of looking into the stands between pitches. I swung at the first pitch a lot. I wasn't too pissed off about making outs, believe me.

Listen, there was a guy who had pitched for the Padres, Ralph Garcia; he was supposed to pitch one game for Mazatlán against Mexicali, and somebody kidnapped him because he wasn't pitching too good. He had pitched the first game of the championship against us and we beat him pretty bad. They didn't want him to pitch again because they were betting on his team, so they kidnapped him.

We were waiting for the game to start, and Garcia just didn't show up. Finally somebody called and said, "He will not pitch tonight. We have kidnapped him. If he even thinks about trying to get away to pitch, we will kill him." All that stuff.

Anyway, after we ended up losing that series, Mazatlán

wanted to add me to their team to play for them in the Caribbean World Series. I didn't have to think about it very long. I didn't even say *"Gracias."* I said, "Fuck, no, I'm going home. I'm outta here." That was as scared as I've ever been playing a baseball game.

After Beaumont, I moved up to Triple-A, which in the Padres organization meant Las Vegas. I played two years there, and, God, it was nice. The place was great. The field was beautiful. We'd go to the shows. The assistant general manager, Don Logan—he's the general manager now—had more connections than any human being around. He'd get us free tickets, free food, whatever. That's why they say that if you're playing in Las Vegas and you get called up to San Diego, you'd probably go, but if it meant going somewhere else, you might want to think about it a little. You might be hesitant about leaving Las Vegas for anyplace else in the major leagues.

When you think about Las Vegas, the first things you think about are the bright lights and the gambling and the tourists. But what I remember most is that the people who live there, who have lived there their whole lives, are the nicest people. I've seen places where the people resented the hell out of the players and what they were doing, but these people were genuinely nice. They were living in a place where you've got all these tourists running through, trying to take over the town. I don't think I could be that nice if I lived there. But they were just great.

The team, on the other hand, was terrible.

We won the first half championship my first year, but we got killed in the playoffs by Hawaii. Hawaii had Bob Walk, Mike Bielecki, and Alfonso Pulido; they each won almost twenty games that year, and that's a lot in the minor leagues. Heck, it's a lot in any league.

I batted .326 that year, but I wasn't disappointed when they sent me back to Las Vegas for the 1985 season. I ended up batting .351, which was good enough to lead the Pacific Coast League that season. But the team was really terrible. We had a lot of injuries. We were shuttling guys in and out from Double-A.

Even coming off that season, there was no guarantee I was going to make the Padres in 1986. I had never gotten called up in September, so I hadn't spent a day in the majors. I batted .465 in spring training, but I still wouldn't have made it if Bobby Brown hadn't decided to retire.

We were playing an exhibition in Las Vegas, and I was expecting to just stay there to start the season. Then Bobby Brown called me aside. He said, "I retired." I asked him why he would do that. He said, "I've got money and I've got other things to do. It's your turn. It's time for you to make your money." And he quit. They were going to keep him instead of me. They had already told him he had made the team.

I didn't know what to say. Do you just say thanks? Or do you say you're sorry that his career is over but yours is just starting? All I know is that it took a pretty big man to do what he did. They had already told him he had made the team and he could have made decent money, but he told them he couldn't do the job for them that I could and that he had a business in Atlantic City and that he was going to retire and let me have my chance.

I see him every once in a while. I was doing a radio show with Harry Kalas, our great announcer, a couple years ago in Atlantic City, and Bobby just walked in. He's a funny man. I'm still grateful for what he did. I don't know what would have happened if I'd been sent back again. But I didn't have to find out. It was time to go to the big leagues.

I ain't an athlete, lady. I'm a baseball player.

FOR AS LONG AS I CAN REMEMBER, I'VE
had to worry about my weight. It hasn't always been the same
worry, though—believe it or not, there was a time when I
worked hard to try to gain weight.

I wanted to play peewee football when I was in the sixth or
seventh grade, but they wouldn't let me. They said I didn't
weigh enough.

I tried and tried and tried to gain weight. I was eating peanut butter and honey all the time. They told me that would help. I'd go out and watch practice and keep eating. I think it was the last two games of the year before I finally weighed enough and they let me play. But I was always there, watching and eating.

Now they're telling me not to eat. I'll tell you, my life has been one extreme or another. West Virginia and New Jersey. San Diego and Philadelphia. Eat and don't eat. It's killing me. I've got to find a happy medium somewhere in this road of life.

I weighed 150 pounds when I got out of high school. Things started changing when I was at Allegany Community College. I was a center fielder back then, and I could run. I think one of the reasons I got drafted was because I could run so well, but I hurt my knee sliding into second to break up a double play while I was playing Class A ball in Reno. And then it started.

For so long I could eat anything I wanted; they kept telling me to put on weight, that I needed to put on weight. That was when I developed my eating habits. Then, after I hurt my knee, I was in a brace for two weeks. I couldn't do much, but I kept right on eating, and I gained fifteen pounds. Quick.

Maybe I would have gained the weight anyway. Everybody in my family started to fill out two or three years after they got out of high school. I did, too. But it didn't bother me then because suddenly I could hit better; I had more power. Then I went to the summer league and I was playing well and I got drafted, so I didn't really think too much about it.

I was in the minor leagues with the Padres when some people in the front office decided that I didn't conform to their standards of what an athlete should look like. It didn't have anything to do with the way I was playing; it was, "Lose weight. You look like hell."

In 1982, at Reno, I hurt my knee again. I did it sliding into second base. I think that's why I still can't slide. I'm leery of it. In spring training, if they ask me to practice sliding, I tell them, hell, I'll just hit home runs instead.

Anyway, my spikes stuck and my knee turned over. I sprained a ligament and they put me back in a brace. And all the time I was in it I ate. I ate hard.

I just kept doing what I'd always done. I ate when it was time to eat. I ate when I was hungry. I ate and I kept on gaining. I never really thought it was a problem until after my second year at Triple-A in Las Vegas; that's when they told me that if I didn't report to spring training the next year at 190 pounds they weren't going to let me do anything until I had lost the weight. I'd be there, but all I'd do would be to work out with the trainer.

So I stayed in Las Vegas and worked out at this clinic. I didn't eat anything. I starved myself. When it came time for the physical and the weigh-in I was at 190 pounds exactly. They let me do what I had to do. I left for Yuma, Arizona, and spring training with Tony Gwynn; he'd had to lose weight, too. And we stopped at Wendy's on the way and had two big double cheeseburgers.

I'm not sure they handled things the best way. Before that, they never really told me anything directly; they just hinted around that I should lose some weight. They tried to tell me some stuff, that the reason I got hurt and missed a couple weeks was because I was too heavy. Well, what had happened was that I hit a ground ball and I was running to first; the first baseman was in the baseline and we collided. He was bent down and I went over him, and when I put out my arm to break my fall I landed on my thumb and it broke. Now, what's that have to do with my weight?

Another time I got hit on the kneecap with a pitch. It cracked the kneecap. Again, that had nothing to do with weight, but they came down and they read the reports, and they saw that I was hurt. And they just said, "Oh, he's hurt. It must be his weight. He's too fat."

But that was the first time they ever said I had to lose weight or I wouldn't play. So I lost it.

And it's been pretty constant ever since then. You just come to the point where you tell people to go to hell. It was a hassle to listen to the same thing every year. It became a pain.

It was especially a pain during spring training in 1992. I had just signed a three-year contract for $7.2 million. It was my first big long-term contract. I guess I should have realized that people would be paying a lot of attention to stuff like my weight. And, I'll admit it, I filled out my uniform pretty good when I got to Clearwater that spring.

Boy, did I take a lot of grief. How much I weighed became a huge deal back in Philadelphia. There were stories in the papers and they talked about it on television and the radio.

To tell you the truth, I didn't like the way I looked any better than anybody else did. Man, I saw a picture someone took. It didn't even look like me; it looked like someone stuck an air hose up my ass and turned it on full blast and left it. I was just enormous. I couldn't wear the pants I'd worn the year before because they were too tight.

Most of the time I try to just let the comments go and not worry about it. I mean, why have a confrontation when you don't have to? But sometimes it just goes too far. And that spring it went too far.

The worst stuff came from one of those all-sports radio stations back in Philadelphia. They started calling doughnut shops in Clearwater, asking the people behind the counter if I had been in there and how many jelly doughnuts I'd bought. That didn't work. Then they started calling this restaurant, Lenny's, where some guys go for breakfast. I've never been in the place in my life, but some waitress got on the phone and started telling everybody what I'd ordered: two omelets, hash browns, four pieces of bacon, toast. *And I've never been in there in my life!*

I don't know. I think you should be judged by what you do. For people to dive into your business like that just doesn't make sense to me. If they think it's going to help their ratings, so be it. But you look at a lot of the guys in that shower room and they're not body beautiful, either. And I look at some of these people who tell me that I'm overweight and I need to lose weight and really ridicule me about it, and they're all fat, too. So what am I supposed to think?

Besides, not too many people realized that when I signed that contract, the Phillies put in a bunch of things that I wasn't allowed to do. One of them was play basketball. I could understand their thinking; they were paying me a lot of money and they didn't want me to go out and get hurt doing something stupid. But I'd always played basketball in the winter to help stay in shape. I wasn't going to go outside and run and freeze to death, so I didn't do anything. It's not an excuse, but it is one reason why I was so heavy that spring.

I don't understand the thinking of some people. Tickets to games aren't cheap, and some guy buys a ticket and comes out to the game just to tell me I'm fat? Why doesn't he just send me a letter? Or a postcard? It would save him a lot of money.

Most of the things people yell at me are the normal stuff: fatass, fat bastard, fat piece of shit, that sort of garbage. But I have to admit, a couple times people have yelled things at me that were kind of amusing.

One time we were at Wrigley Field in Chicago, and when you play outfield those bleacher bums are always on you. So I was out there and one guy yelled, "If you hauled ass, you'd have to make two trips." I liked that. I thought it was pretty good.

When I was playing for Las Vegas, the Pacific Coast League still had a team in Hawaii. We'd go out there and play eight or twelve games in one trip to Aloha Stadium to cut down on travel expenses. The place was always empty. Nobody ever went to watch the games, which is probably why they don't have a team there anymore, but it's a big stadium, and if there aren't many people in a big stadium and one guy yells, his voice echoes so you can hear him all over the stadium.

Well, we're over there and I was heavy, as heavy as I've ever been. This one guy was on me hard all night long. Late in the game he yelled, "Hey, Kruk, I finally realized why you wear number eight." Now, everyone could hear him. I was in the dugout. I could hear him. The players on the field heard him. They all started laughing. What few fans there were, they could all hear him.

And he yelled, "It's because to get that way you *ate* and you *ate* and you *ate* and you *ate*." I have to admit, that was a pretty good one. It was clever. And besides, here's a guy who lives in paradise and he came out to the game just to yell at me. It made me feel kind of special. He's spending his spare time in Aloha Stadium when he could be doing something else in Hawaii. Hell, we wished we were doing something else in Hawaii instead of playing ball, because we got killed all the time. I thought, that man is either bored to death or he hates this beautiful place. He must be a miserable son of a gun. But that was still pretty clever.

Then when I was in San Diego, still wearing number 8, Tim Flannery said I was the only guy he knew who wore his silhouette on the back of his uniform. That was a pretty good one. I mean, Tim isn't skinny, either. So that was pretty good.

Maybe that's why I've changed my number so many times.

Around the Phillies, I answer to Jake. They started calling me that after the guy on cable who does "Body by Jake." That's pretty funny, too.

The thing is, it shouldn't matter what you look like as long as you're doing the job. I'm not trying to run a marathon; I just have to run the bases and they're only ninety feet apart. Mainly, I have to hit a baseball.

There's a story, a funny story, about me sitting in a restaurant. I'm eating this big meal and maybe having a couple beers. A woman comes by the table. She recognizes me and she's, you know, shocked because it seems like I should be in training or something. She's getting all over me, saying that a professional athlete should take better care of himself.

I lean back and I say to her, "I ain't an athlete, lady. I'm a baseball player."

That pretty much sums it up. The only problem is, I don't remember ever saying that. I could have, but I don't remember it. Randy Ready started the story and he swears it's true, that he was with me when it happened.

After saying all that, I have to admit that I have tried really hard to lose weight in the past. The last two off-seasons, I've made a real effort to get into better shape.

Two years ago, after the 1992 season, I had to have shoulder surgery. That didn't have anything to do with my weight either, but I did have this operation. They called it "tightening the capsule." To me it was more like they ripped my shoulder open, sewed up a big hole, drilled three holes in the bones and attached some stuff. But the thing I remembered most was that the team physician, Dr. Phillip Marone, told me that hopefully I'd be able to swing a bat by spring training. *Hopefully.* That scared me.

What made it worse was that my brother Joe had gone through the same thing. Several years ago when he was a basketball coach in North Carolina he tried to dunk a volleyball and he caught his arm on the rim. He ripped some stuff in his shoulder and he still can't raise that arm above shoulder level.

Instead of going home that winter, I stayed in Philadelphia. I went to Veterans Stadium five days a week and worked with our trainer, Jeff Cooper. I was doing pretty good at keeping my weight under control. Then I went home for Thanksgiving. I came back and I didn't do quite as good. I went home for Christmas and it was all over.

I disappointed myself. But I just got to the point where I couldn't stay on a diet anymore. Philadelphia is nice and all, but it's not home. I'm gone more than eight months of the year anyway, and I just wanted to go home. That's where my family and most of my friends are, and that's where I wanted to be. While I was home I did the exercises for my arm, but I didn't have Coop there every day nagging me: "What did you eat today? You can't have that. Let's eat this." It wasn't his fault. It was nobody's fault but mine.

I did enough exercises so that my shoulder was fine, and that was the main thing I was worried about. I know that if I'm heavy I can still play, but if I'm hurt, if I can't swing the bat, I can't play, and that would kill me. I was worried more about my shoulder than my weight. And by the time I went to Florida, I had gained back the weight I lost.

It was kind of like a couple years before, when I had arthroscopic knee surgery. The Phillies wanted me to stay around after the operation and work out. I did, for a while, then I quit. I thought I had had enough and I went home.

But I paid for that. The last couple years, my back has been hurting. The doctors said it's because I'm too heavy. I can understand that. Pain, like pain in your knees, you can tolerate that. But when your back hurts, it's just miserable. You're just a miserable person. The Phillies asked me if I wanted to go to New Orleans and work out with Mackie Shilstone for a couple weeks in January. He's a conditioning guy who was hired by the Phillies. He also had players from other teams working out last winter. I said that I would do it, not because I was going to look better, or whatever; for the first time I really wanted to do it because it was going to help my back.

Before, well, sometimes the more people tell you something,

the more you don't want to do it. Maybe I just didn't like the way they put it: "You're fat. Lose weight." Nobody ever really sat me down and explained why losing some weight might be the best thing for me.

Last season I talked to Darren Daulton a lot about it. You know how he is, a fanatic about fitness and working out and all that. When you hear it from a guy who's a friend, a peer, you take it a little different than if it's coming from a guy who's sitting in an office all day.

Anyway, when the Phillies made the suggestion about going to New Orleans I wasn't opposed to it. I went down there for a week of preliminary tests in November. The first day I went to a doctor and he gave me all these blood tests. They found out all the bad stuff that was in my body, the cholesterol and all that crap, stuff I didn't even know what they were talking about. They gave me a diet plan and showed me some exercises to help strengthen my stomach muscles, which would help make my back feel better.

They showed me all these exercises that I had to do with a cord, exercises where I'd simulate doing baseball things, like swinging a bat and bending down to field a ground ball. The idea was that when I got to Florida I wouldn't be as sore as I had been in some recent years. I mean, there were days when I wished I didn't have to play. There were days I'd come in and I was so sore that I was praying I wouldn't be in the lineup. I'd never been like that before.

As it turned out, I didn't go back to New Orleans for the final program. It was turning into a media circus and I didn't want that. ESPN wanted to follow me around. I don't like being followed. But I did keep doing the exercises and riding the exercise bike. My back didn't hurt anymore, and that was the point in the first place.

I got the program. I'm not a child. I'm not stupid. I know I have to do the exercises because I have a bad back. But why do I have to go down there and have people looking over my shoulder? Do this. Do that. If I want to do it, I'm going to do it; if I don't, I'm not. But it's my back and I know it hurts and I know I have to do exercises to help it. I'm not doing it for the Phillies or Mackie Shilstone; I'm doing it for me. Because when I'm done playing, I still want to be able to walk. I still want to be able to stand upright.

At least sometimes. Probably not as often as now.

But I'm always going to have a bad back. It's not just for baseball. It's for the rest of my life.

Before the 1993 season, I had a lot of trouble. The fields are hard and it just seemed like every muscle in my legs hurt. No matter how much I stretched, it didn't help. Some days we had to run after the workout, and I was so sore I was hoping I'd break a leg just so I wouldn't have to run. And that's something that I know has to do with being heavy.

I know I'm not the most diligent worker in the winter. When I come to spring training, that's the first time I pick up a ball and a bat. I don't throw in the winter. So when you take four months off and then you go right back and start using those baseball muscles, you're going to get bad sore. I guess that's why I look like hell sometimes.

So that's another reason why I wanted to go into spring training in better condition this year. The last couple years I'd had to play nine innings almost every day, make all the trips. It wasn't Jim Fregosi's fault; he had to play me into shape. But I didn't want to go through that again. Besides, you don't want to use up all your hits in spring training. There are only so many bullets left in the gun. You can't waste them on target practice.

The other thing is that, as you get older, aches and pains become pulls and strains. Goose Gossage told me that. It's depressing. But I have to work on something that always came naturally to me. I've seen those Advil commercials Nolan Ryan does on television. I'm not in as good shape as Nolan Ryan is

—and I'm not as old. But he's right about having to work harder as you get older.

It's not easy. I know that. I've lost weight before, but keeping it off is a whole different deal.

There are times during the winter when I'm out on my farm. Maybe I don't want to go all the way back home to eat that crappy food, you know, the bland stuff with no salt and no spices, that horrible stuff? Every once in a while, maybe I'll have a burger instead. What the hell—one burger a week can't kill you. If it could, I'd have been dead a long time ago.

I've gone through this so many times. A week before spring training I'll say, "All right, this is it. I'm not going to eat red meat. I'm not going to eat fried foods." Then I go to Florida. I'm going to get my exercise, so I go out to play golf. Then I'm done playing, I haven't eaten all day, and what is there to eat at a golf course? Why, hamburgers and hot dogs. So you're right back at it.

Or say we have a day game. What I used to do is come to the clubhouse, and for breakfast I'd have a couple hot dogs. Cut them up into pieces, put some mustard and ketchup on them, and eat them. Now, I know that's not the breakfast of champions. But you come into the clubhouse early and what do they have? Doughnuts. *That's* pretty healthy. So I throw a couple hot dogs in the microwave.

That's the hardest thing during the season, that you eat out so much. It's tough to go to a restaurant and order something and then say that you want it cooked this way and leave off the seasoning and leave off the sauce. The thing to do is just go in and ask for the most bland thing they have. I figure it's probably good for me. Because it sucks.

The best diet is just to go into a restaurant and say, "Give me the thing on your menu that tastes the worst." It'll probably be good for you because that's what everything else I've eaten that's supposed to be good for me tastes like.

I guess a lot of people are on diets and that's my best advice:

eat bad food. If it tastes good, spit it out, because it's not going to help you. I mean, you can eat chicken—but you can't fry it. You can have a potato, but no butter. No salt, no spices. So everything is bland. It's a terrible thing.

I had to have something to snack on, so I got these no-fat potato chips. I took one bite and gave them to the dogs. The dogs wouldn't eat them. Ran from them.

Everything they had me eating in New Orleans tasted like cardboard. It's like getting a big fancy package in the mail in a big box. Then you take it out and eat the box.

I suppose you could walk out in the garden and chew the dirt, but there's probably fat in the dirt. It's no fun. I wish I had never gotten overweight. I wish I had stayed reasonable. But that didn't happen and now I really have to work at it.

Every once in a while you get some good news. Like after I got home from New Orleans, Dave Hollins called me and asked how everything went. I told him it went great but that I was on this fat-free diet and they wanted me to cut out beer. They wanted me to cut out red meat and fatty foods. And I told him I'd like to have a beer every once in a while and a steak, but apparently I can't.

Well, Dave's on a health kick. He's into all that stuff. And that's when he dropped it on me: Coors Light has no fat. He told me to look at the label. I didn't even know beer had a label, like cereal or something. Sure enough, though, I looked and he was right.

So I had to switch from Budweiser to Coors Light, because I can only have so much fat in my diet. At least it's something. Even more important, if I didn't switch, Dave might kill me.

Eating peanut butter and honey to try to gain weight? Those were the days.

We were a pretty undernourished team. He destroyed a lot of those postgame spreads.

I WAS SITTING THERE GETTING READY TO start my first big league spring training camp with the Padres. It was Yuma, Arizona, in 1986. I was nervous as hell to begin with. We were in the clubhouse and somebody came out and said to sit down, we were going to have a meeting, the manager would be right out.

Now, the manager was Dick Williams. I mean, it was supposed to be Dick Williams. We kept expecting him to come out, but he never showed up. He had decided to quit, but he accidentally forgot to tell them he was quitting. So we sat there for a while and we didn't have a manager. Then we went outside and we sat there for about an hour, and the manager still didn't show up. Somebody came along and said we should do some exercises, hit, and do some running, and they hoped they could find a coach to come out and hit us some grounders because they didn't know where the manager was.

Welcome to the big leagues. I said, "This could be a fucked-up career right here."

It turned out to be even worse than we realized. A day or two later they named Steve Boros the manager. Now, he's a nice man. He might be the nicest man in the world. And that was the problem. He was *too* nice.

I've been around long enough now that I've played for quite a few managers. One thing I've noticed is that whenever teams change managers, they usually try to get somebody who's exactly the opposite of what they had before. Dick Williams was too tough, so they hired Steve Boros. He was too nice, so they hired Larry Bowa to make sure we wouldn't get away with anything. It's culture shock is what it is.

They never really gave the manager a chance in San Diego. They went from Dick Williams, who is a lot like Larry, to the nicest guy in the world. Then they hired Larry, another psychotic. Then they went to Jack McKeon, who was basically a nice guy. Bad, nice, bad, nice. That's tough. That's too much of a roller coaster for players to handle.

Steve Boros lasted just that one year. And in that time I never saw him get mad. He had the weirdest way of getting thrown out of a game I've ever seen. Steve Garvey, who was finishing his career with the Padres, got tossed one night, for the first time ever. The funny thing was, he didn't do anything; he was on deck when Bip Roberts was coming in to score, and they called him out. Bip threw his helmet and said some things. Garvey was walking to the plate to go to bat and the umpire thought he had said it, so they threw Garvey out of the game.

Next day they were at home plate exchanging the lineup cards, and Boros pulled a videotape out of his jacket pocket. He said, "Here, watch this. If you do you'll see Garvey didn't say anything." And they ran him right there.

The players didn't know Boros was going to do that. It was like, "Wow, we didn't know he had that in him." I think that's about the maddest he ever got. He'd go out and argue, but he wouldn't yell or anything. It was like he was having a conversation with the umpire. How could you kick a guy out like that? That was his only fault as a manager that I could see—he was just too nice.

That wasn't Larry Bowa's problem.

If they wanted to go in the opposite direction, they got the perfect guy. A helluva coach. A great field manager. God, what a dickhead. I thought he was the biggest asshole in the United States of America. Of course, there are still days when I think that, but only some days. Not every day like before.

Oh, yeah, one more thing. The best thing that happened to me in my career was him becoming my manager.

Larry brought me in and he taught me. When Garvey got hurt during the '87 season, Bowa told me he didn't give a fuck what anybody said, that I was going to play first base every day. I don't think the front office really liked that. I think he had his hands tied in a lot of ways, that he wasn't allowed to do what he really wanted to do. That wasn't fair to him and I think it really pissed him off. But he said, "I don't care, they can fire me, they can do whatever they want. But you're playing." And that's exactly the way it was. Until he was fired, I played every day. And as soon as he left, my playing time started to dwindle, until by the time I was traded, I was playing about once a week.

I liked playing for Bowa because I knew that if I screwed

up, he was going to call me in and yell at me. Somebody even put my name up over his office door because I was in there getting yelled at so often. God, we'd fight. It was my second year in the big leagues and he'd tell me to go tell so-and-so who's been around ten years to do this or that. I'd yell back, "That ain't my job. That's yours. If you want something told, you go tell him."

He was such a pain in the ass, you just didn't want to hear it. If I did something wrong, if I made a mental mistake, he'd call me in and air me out. These days he just gives me little shots, but back then it was fifteen minutes of him cursing me out and then I'd go out and play. These days he just gives me a little "What the hell were you doing on that play?" or "What the fuck was going through your mind?" Little things like that. It adds up and you want to kill him. But you also know that he's right.

We had some good ones. But we never lost respect for each other, and if it wasn't for him, and I might never have gotten a chance to play every day in the big leagues, and I might never have gotten out of San Diego. Bowa thought I had potential and he wanted me to live up to it. I just wasn't quite smart enough to realize it at the time.

Not all of the guys took it that way, though. He came out the first day he was manager in spring training and he started talking about what it was going to be like. He probably didn't know half the guys on the team. He just started talking. We're going to stress fundamentals, we're going to get into shape, we're going to run hard, we're going to do all our drills, everybody is going to work his ass off. And he just kept going and going and building and building. Pretty soon he's yelling. Now, I wasn't surprised. I had been sent back to Las Vegas for six days the year before when they traded for Randy Ready. Bowa was the manager there and it didn't take me all six days to realize he was going to be a little different from Steve Boros.

But some of the older guys were looking at each other. "Damn, first day. Fuck this guy, he ain't going to be around long." Well, he wasn't. We didn't play good. But the reason we didn't play good was because we weren't a good team and nothing he did was going to make us a good team. If you can't take a little yelling, you're a bad sport.

The funniest thing I ever saw Larry Bowa do he denies, but it's true. He called a team meeting in St. Louis and he was really pissed. He thought guys were playing bad on purpose to try to get him fired. He thought if somebody made an error or if somebody struck out, it was because of him. It wasn't because you just missed the ball or the guy made a good pitch; you were doing it on purpose to get him.

We had this meeting, and he was yelling so bad he was foaming at the mouth and he started to shake. His face was red and the veins were popping out. And he bent over and grabbed his ass and spread it. He screamed, "You're fucking me right in the ass!" Benito Santiago started laughing. I mean, you couldn't help yourself. It was hilarious. Bowa just went into his office and slammed the door.

Another time, he snapped after a game in Cincinnati. He went into a tirade. He picked up a fungo bat and shattered it on the water cooler in the dugout. I mean *shattered* it. Then he came up into the clubhouse and he was throwing things everywhere.

The amazing thing was, through the whole thing our hitting coach, Deacon Jones, was sound asleep. He had some kind of condition that caused him to sleep a lot. I mean, this tantrum was high up on the Richter scale, and Deacon Jones was asleep in his locker. Tony Gwynn was in the locker next to me. We knew that after a loss we shouldn't undress right away. The only things we took off were our gloves and our hats and we'd sit there and wait for Bowa. God forbid that you'd leave your locker. Because you knew. At first guys would come in and do what they had to do—eat the spread or take a shower or whatever. But a month or two into the season it was come in, sit down, and wait. And Bowa would have a little tirade. He'd go into his office and then he'd come back out and start going nuts.

I could see where some of the older guys might have thought it was entertaining. But it scared me to death.

Anyway, that one day Bowa comes out and he's yelling and Deacon Jones is sound asleep. It's hard not to laugh when a man is going off like that, let me tell you.

Sometimes Bowa would have a long snap, but this was a short one. He yelled and screamed for a minute or so. Then he broke a bat and yelled and screamed some more. Then he went into his office and slammed the door. It was like maybe a bomb goes off and you sleep through it, but then a mouse creeps through your room and you wake up. That's what it was like with Deacon Jones; he just woke up all of a sudden and got undressed like everybody else. He never knew what happened. He was oblivious to it all.

Another good story about Deacon: We were in Denver for an exhibition game against the Cubs. I was struggling. Bowa had already come out in the paper and said if I wasn't hitting, I wasn't playing, since it wasn't like I was out there for defensive purposes. So Carmelo Martinez was playing a lot more than I was.

First game in Denver, I don't think I got a hit. I came back into the dugout after one at bat and I sat down next to Deacon so I could talk to him. I said, "Hey, Deacon, what the hell am I doing wrong?" And I didn't get an answer. I said, "Deacon!" I leaned over and asked him again. And he was sleeping. During the game.

Don't get me wrong. He was a great hitting coach and I learned a lot from him. But when he decided it was time to sleep, he slept. In a way, I kind of envy him, because there are times I'd like to sleep and I can't.

I hope Bowa gets another chance to manage. I think he's learned a lot. There might have only been five or six guys who played for him in San Diego that were grateful for the experience. The other guys probably wanted to kill him. But I'll never say a bad word about him.

I don't think our general manager, Jack McKeon, much liked the way Bowa snapped, the way he yelled at fans above the dugout at home. I think McKeon wanted everybody to fit into San Diego, nice and laid-back. Don't get upset. Whatever happens, happens. Larry wasn't like that. If something happened there had to be a reason and he was damn sure going to find out what it was. He was going to find out right then. And if he didn't like what he found out, he was going to have a meeting and yell and throw things and turn over the postgame spread.

We were a pretty undernourished team. He destroyed a lot of those postgame spreads.

There was one time in spring training when we got beat. Now, San Diego to Yuma is only a two-hour drive, so on the weekends a lot of people would come out to watch us play. We were winning going into the later innings, but you know how spring training games are—you play the regulars five or six innings, then you play the guys who are trying to make the team. That's just the way it is. Back then I didn't care for it. Now I really love it.

Anyway, we had some younger guys in the game and they made a couple errors and we ended up losing the game.

Bowa was nice and calm. I think he realized that he had some guys in there who weren't going to make the team. So they made a couple errors. No big deal. He was standing on the foul line while we were running our sprints after the game. He was joking around and laughing. But then an older woman, a season ticket holder from San Diego, starts yelling at him: "It wasn't their fault, Larry. You don't have to punish them. It was your fault, you put all those guys in the game."

Well, being the little psychopath competitor that he is, he turned around and hollered, "Why don't you shut the fuck up, you old bitch?"

The whole place went real quiet. I think he got reprimanded for that. He apologized to the woman later.

So I think Jack McKeon may have thought Bowa was losing control. We heard that Jack wanted to step in and smooth things out between Larry and some of the veterans, but Larry wouldn't allow it. It was his team; if he wanted to have a meeting, he would have his own meeting. He thought the way to save his job was to be himself. And it didn't work. We weren't playing good and Jack probably made some suggestions: play this guy, give that guy a rest. Larry had a couple guys, and I was one of them, that Jack really didn't want to see in there too much. So Jack fired him and made himself manager.

But Jack had it tough. That's a hard switch to make. One day you're negotiating contracts, trying to lowball a guy, to sign the guy for the lowest possible price. You tell him that's all he's worth. Then, the next thing, you're the manager. You're trying to be rah-rah. You're telling everybody what a great player he is. But the player is sitting there thinking, "If I'm such a great player, how come you tried to screw me on my contract and not give me any more money?" It really didn't work out.

It's different managing in the big leagues than it is in the minors. My first year in Walla Walla, the manager we had was crazy. Bill Bryk. He's a cross-checker scout for the Pirates now. He was a comedian. He was so funny that I think he was on "Saturday Night Live" once. He was in a skit cast as the manager having a meeting with the regulars on the show. He had a great sense of humor.

He was a perfect manager for me to start out with. I was intimidated just to be there, a guy from a small junior college going to play with all these guys who went to four-year schools in California and everywhere else. If Bowa had been my manager I might not have made it. I couldn't have handled it. But Bill Bryk let us play. He knew we were young and probably scared to death.

He tried to make it enjoyable. He'd joke around. He knew that if you made a mistake or made an error, you probably thought they were going to release you. At that point, you think you have to play a perfect game every day—at least that's the way I felt. But he'd say, "Fuck it. Don't worry about it. You ain't the first player to make a mistake. A lot better players than you have made errors."

My manager at Reno and Beaumont was Jack Maloof. He was real religious, real quiet. He was also a real good hitting coach. If he hadn't worked with me and changed some things about the way I hit, I probably wouldn't have made it. There have been a lot of people like that along the way.

Jack was a born-again Christian. He never tried to put that on anyone; he kept to himself. But he could be tough, too. You might think, he's a religious guy, you could take advantage of him. Maybe miss curfew. Didn't work. He'd fine you in a second. Then you might think that because he was a nice guy, you could talk him out of it. We all tried it. Couldn't do it.

Then in Las Vegas I had Bob Cluck for two years. He was the first manager I had who said, "Just go and do what you want." What he meant was to have fun when you played. The Padres did me a favor when they drafted me and I don't want to say nothing bad about anyone, but up to that point with them it was like you were still on a college team. Do this, do that. Curfews and all that shit. We had our guidelines, and if you stepped over them you got reprimanded.

And then there was Bob Cluck.

We were playing bad one day. He called a team meeting after the game. He didn't curse or anything; he just said, "I'll be sitting in the lobby. And anybody who comes in before four o'clock will be fined. Go out and do whatever you have to do because we suck. Get it all out of your system." And we did it. I thought, "Man, this is fun."

It wasn't do this and do that and be a good boy and be in bed by nine. You know? He let us be men. Physically, we were men, of course, but mentally, we were still kids. And kids like to do mischievous things and have fun.

But this guy was one of us. He was like a kid. He just enjoyed watching us play. He loved what he was doing. Some guys had been around baseball a long time; maybe they weren't progressing and didn't think they were getting a chance to make it to the big leagues as a coach or something, so they were bitter.

Cluck wasn't like that. He was one of the first ones to the park and one of the last to leave. You could tell him anything. He'd tell you anything. It was like playing on a summer team where you have a player-coach. That's what it was like.

After he told us anybody who came in before four o'clock would be fined, we had a day game the next day. We got killed. Anybody who showed up played. We had the biggest outfield, weight-wise, in the history of baseball. Joe Lansford was in left. He weighed about 230. I was going about 230 then. And Rick Lancellotti was about 220, 225. None of us could run. We weren't exactly cutting off the gaps that day.

Anyway, then I went to the big leagues. I played for Steve Boros and I played for Larry Bowa. Then Jack McKeon took over, and we didn't see eye to eye. He had his boys, and if you weren't one of his boys, you were not going to excel in his system.

In the meantime, Bowa had been hired as the Phillies third base coach. Even before that, I knew he was talking me up. We were in New York when he got fired. Two or three days later we were in Philly. He was out on the field doing an interview and he said, "You're coming with me, bitch." I said, "Man, the quicker the better because I don't think I can do this." It took a year, but he helped get me out of there.

When I got to Philadelphia, Nick Leyva was the manager. He was a young guy, getting his first chance. Lee Thomas had hired him because Nick was the third base coach when they were both with the Cardinals. I said earlier that when teams change managers they usually go from one extreme to another. The same thing happened when I started out with the Phillies, except that Nick was the manager the whole time.

From the time I was traded there to the end of the year, he kind of kept his distance. We'd go out to the field and he'd sit in his office; we'd take batting practice and come back in and he'd still be in his office. We'd go to play the game and he'd be in the dugout. I never really got a feel for the man from talking to him or anything like that.

Some guys ripped him at the end of the year, so the next spring he was coming around, slapping people on the back and telling jokes. You can't do that. They ask the players to be consistent. The manager has to be consistent, too.

People may think that since players make all this money, and a lot of us have long-term contracts, that the manager shouldn't make that much difference to us. But he does. Players look to the manager to set the tone.

All you can really ask from a manager is not to be a Jekyll and Hyde. I know it's hard; a manager has to deal with twenty-five of us and we've only got to deal with one of him. But Leyva started out really distant, and then when guys ripped him he went home over the winter and said to himself, "I've got to be nice. They're ripping me and I've got to be nice and change their minds." Well, that doesn't happen. What happens is that guys think, "I ripped him and he's being nice to me. So I can rip him all I want." You lose respect for a manager that way.

The other thing was, he was a young manager. He was trying to get along. He was trying to keep his job. And one time that meant sitting me down.

We were playing in Dodger Stadium. I grounded out or something, probably a 22-hopper to second on a pitch I thought I should have hit. So I took a right turn and before I got into the dugout I yelled an obscenity that begins with F. Real loud.

Nothing was said at the time, but when I came in the next day I wasn't in the lineup, even though the Dodgers had a right-handed pitcher starting. I asked Denis Menke, our hitting coach, how come I wasn't playing. He just gave me this funny look and said, you know, maybe I should ask Nick. I asked Menke if he knew why. He said, "Yeah, but I'm not going to tell you because you'll just get pissed off."

Well, what the hell? I didn't do nothing. I wasn't out all night. It's not like Leyva saw me come into the hotel at seven in the morning, drunk, with four women. Menke said if he was me he wouldn't even ask. Just take the day off and go from there. I asked another coach. I won't name him, but you know how Bowa likes to stir things up. And he told me it was because I had cursed. I said, "You gotta be shittin' me."

Somebody had been watching the game on television back in Philadelphia and heard me curse. So I had to sit out a game. I was told later that I wasn't supposed to play, no matter what. But that turned out to be the night we were behind, 11–1, going into the eighth inning. Then we had a big comeback and we ended up winning, 12–11. I think it got to a point in the ninth inning where they had to use me or let the pitcher bat. If Leyva had disciplined me that bad, having me sit while he let the pitcher bat, I'd have walked out. And I never walk out on anything. I talked to him later. I said, "Am I the only guy who ever cursed on the field?" I said, "If you're going to sit out everyone for cursing on the field, hell, Dale Murphy will be out there all by himself." I just didn't understand it. It was stupid.

I think it came from above him. But Leyva went along with it, and he shouldn't have.

By the way, I hit a three-run homer to tie the game in the ninth.

That was one of the first things I talked to Jim Fregosi about when they hired him to replace Leyva. I asked him if I would be benched for cursing. He said I wouldn't.

I appreciated that.

Nick got fired thirteen games into the 1991 season, his third year. Some people thought he didn't get a chance, but I thought by then it was something that had to be done. It had just gotten to a point where, I don't want to say we didn't like playing for him, but we just didn't understand him. We were bad the year before and we'd gotten off to another bad start. Lee Thomas thought he had put together a pretty good team. He thought we should be doing better, and the pressure was on. And I think he just figured you can't fire all the players, as much as he would have liked to get rid of some of us. Plus Nick just seemed to grow a little more distant every year. By the end, it was like the patients were running the asylum.

A perfect example came early that year. We'd opened the season on the road, three games in New York. Then we had an off-day. Our home opener was on a Friday night against St. Louis at Vet. On the wall of the clubhouse, right next to the double doors of the tunnel that lead to the field, is a board where they post the lineup for that night's game. When we came in, that lineup had Steve Lake catching.

Darren Daulton came in and saw that right away. The Cardinals had a left-hander, Jamie Moyer, starting, but still, Darren was supposed to be our everyday catcher. It was the first week of the season and we'd been off the day before, so he wasn't tired. It didn't make sense. Darren went into Nick's office and closed the door. A couple minutes later he came out and the lineup was changed. He started.

It was pretty apparent this was not a good situation.

No matter what anybody thinks, you look to your manager to have some kind of control. When all bedlam breaks loose, you want a calming guy, a guy who can step in and say, "Listen, this is the way it is." But when something like that lineup change happens, you don't know what to think. We joked to Darren that maybe he was really running the team. And I think some guys lost even more respect for Nick then. He just lost control at the end. He was trying to be tough, but it's tough to be tough when the players know they can probably talk you out of something.

Fregosi is just the opposite. He comes off as a nice guy—friendly, but you don't cross him and you can't change his mind. Not that we haven't tried. I can't tell you how many times he's come out to the mound to make a pitching change, and he'll call for the new pitcher, and Darren and I will stand there and say, "What the fuck are you bringing *that* guy in for? What the hell are you thinking about?" And Fregosi just smiles and says, "Because that's what I want to do" or "I don't know. I just hope it works." It's his decision. He isn't going to argue about it.

Every day I'm not playing, I go into his office. "I want to play today. I can hit this guy. I'm tired of sitting. I feel good." And he'll just sit there and nod his head. Then I say, "Okay, then, I'm going to play? I'm in the lineup?"

And he says, "Nope." And that's it. You don't push it any further, because he's the boss.

He's kind of like a father after all the kids have grown up and they come back for Christmas. It's like my father when me and my three brothers tell jokes and they make fun of something that happened during the season. My dad just sits back and watches and doesn't say much. That's the way Fregosi is. But if you're from the outside and you try to dig into it, you better watch out. He'll come down on you hard.

See, Fregosi did everything we've done back when he played.

Probably more. He's heard all the excuses. He probably used them himself. He knows what we go through and he hasn't forgotten.

Some guys forget. I think Bowa may have forgotten a little; he put in rules and stuff that he probably would've bitched about when he was playing. But I think Fregosi probably told himself when he was a player that if he was ever a manager he wouldn't do that, and he doesn't.

Fregosi doesn't worry about the little things. He doesn't let the front office tell him how we should behave on the field. He lets us be us.

Sometimes you just snap and then you feel fine. Once at the Vet I went up the tunnel to the clubhouse, and when I got there I only had a little bit of my bat left in my hand and my batting helmet had exploded. All the stuff in my locker got tossed. I've destroyed toilets, too. They make easy targets. They're sitting right there and you know if you hit them they're going to break.

It's bad when you hit a wall, though. When you hit something solid with your bat it really stings. Then you're even more pissed off. One time I tried to break my helmet. I threw it against the wall three times and it wouldn't break. I just kept getting madder and madder. I got so mad that I went and got my bat and pounded on the helmet until it broke. By that time I was more pissed off at the helmet for not breaking than I was about the at bat I had just had.

I hate schedules. Never liked them. I don't like it when I have to be here at a certain time, do that at a certain time, people always telling me what to do. I always just figured that when you got there, that's when you arrived.

Maybe that got me in trouble with some managers. But with Fregosi, it's pretty simple. The game starts at 7:35. Before that there's batting practice, and guys who play every day hit in their group. But if you don't feel like it, if you feel like all you need to get ready is five swings, fine. Or when my back was bothering me, if it stiffened up and I didn't want to take infield, that was no problem. A lot of managers would have said, "Go take a hundred grounders." Fregosi just let us be us.

It was our clubhouse. He had his office, and the coaches had their office. The clubhouse was ours. If something happened, we dealt with it there. We didn't drag it into the newspapers. At least we tried not to. Sometimes, I'm sorry to say, that's the only way to get through to some guys. But for the most part, we'd handle it in our own house. To tell the truth, that's where we lived most of the time.

If something went on that we didn't like, we straightened it out. We didn't need a manager or coaches to help us. And I think we respected each other more for it. I could walk up to somebody and say, "I don't like the way you're approaching this." And he could do the same to me. We police ourselves. It gets hairy sometimes, but Fregosi lets us do it.

At the same time he knows where to draw the line. He plays cards with us, but we don't step into his territory.

Here's an example. A couple years ago we lost a game in Pittsburgh. Fregosi made some moves during the game that didn't work out. It was just one of those games where we used seven pitchers and a bunch of pinch-hitters, and every time he made a move it sort of backfired. I don't remember exactly what the moves were, just that nothing seemed to work that night. We ended up losing the game in twelve innings. After the media left the clubhouse, we sat in the trainer's room for a couple hours, had a few beers. We just thought Fregosi had made some bad moves. We kind of criticized him.

That's the thing about our team. When it comes time to rip people, no one's pardoned. Even the manager.

He understands that. But there's a limit, too. I guess the speaker phones must have been on, because when we came in the next day he called us into his office. He said, "I get paid to manage this team. You get paid to play. You guys aren't perfect, either. I make mistakes. I admit it. But if you've got something to say to me, you come in here and tell it to me to my face. Then we'll talk about it. But don't sit there and talk behind my back." And he was right. We were wrong and we didn't do it again.

Fregosi and Bowa are the two best managers I've played for in the way they handle situations on the field. On our team, Lenny Dykstra and Mariano Duncan can run and that's about it, so we have to hit. In San Diego when Bowa was managing, Tony Gwynn could hit, I could hit, and Randy Ready could hit. Benito Santiago had a great rookie year, but no one else really came through and played the way they were capable of playing. So Bowa had to go for the bunt, he had to hit-and-run. But he didn't get outmanaged. He and Fregosi are similar in that way.

What sets Fregosi apart is how he deals with people. When he calls you into his office, it's like sitting down and talking to your grandfather. You just walk in and ask what the hell he wants and he tells you. He's all nice, and when you leave you think, God, that was easy. With Bowa, though, you were all white-knuckled when the clubhouse guy said the manager wanted to see you. You could end up dropping each other right there. But that's the only difference between the two. And I think Bowa would be a lot better at communicating now.

People always want to talk about the manager knowing strategy, but the manager doesn't dictate that, the players do. In a tie game, bottom of the ninth, say a guy gets on. You have your third, fourth, or fifth hitter coming up—some guy who has probably never bunted in his life. So why put the bunt on?

I think managers take the heat for that from fans, who think you should bunt all the time. But wouldn't you rather have those guys swinging instead of trying to bunt? And that's what makes a good manager, knowing the players and what they can do.

I know when I go up, if there's a guy on first in a tie game or if we're losing by a run at home in the late innings, I'll never look for a bunt. I might look for a hit-and-run or a steal, but I know they won't make me bunt—because they know I can't.

Some managers have egos. They want to run the whole show, and they expect a hitter in the middle of the order to bunt. But that doesn't make sense.

I've seen managers bunt their fourth hitter because that's what the book says, that you've got to get the tying or winning run into scoring position with less than two outs. Well, if you have a runner at first base with your fourth hitter up, he's *in* scoring position. That bastard at the plate is supposed to be able to hit balls into the gap and hit balls over the fence; why else is he batting fourth? Why take the bat out of his hands?

Say you bunt your third hitter in a tie game because your two-hole hitter led off and got on base. And say your third hitter gets a good bunt down and gets the guy over. Everybody says he did his job. Well, right. But he takes the bat out of the fourth hitter's hands, because they're going to walk him. So you're not giving a chance to two guys who are supposed to be your best hitters.

We work on bunting and all that stuff in spring training, but we don't use it during the season because Fregosi plays to our strengths. He uses his strategy *toward* us, not against us. He knows I can't bunt. He knows Dave Hollins can bunt left-handed but not right-handed. Fregosi's the perfect gambler as a manager.

We might lose a game and people will say, "Why didn't he bunt?" I ain't going to lie; I've said it, too. But when you really think about it, you can see why he played it the way he did.

So, yes, a manager makes a difference. But he still can't hit or pitch for you.

If the count goes 0–2 too many times, that's when you find yourself back playing in the Sunday afternoon beer leagues.

BASEBALL PLAYERS TEND TO THINK THAT

if you can hit a baseball, you can do anything. Ted Williams used to say it's the hardest thing to do in all of sports. Pitchers throw so hard that your reaction time is unbelievably short. So we think we're invincible. We know our reactions are good and that we can get out of any tough situation.

It don't work that way. Just hitting the ball is hard enough. Hitting it where nobody can catch it is another story.

Also, maybe in the back of your mind you're thinking that if the ball hits me in the wrist or it hits me in the head, I might never be the same again. Yeah, major leaguers think about that. It's scary. But it's part of the consequences of your job.

For me, hitting means studying tapes. The Phillies have a guy, Video Dan Stephenson, who does a great job of getting videotapes of just about all the pitchers in the league, so we can go back and watch what pitches they throw, how they work hitters, if they throw a trick pitch, that sort of thing. I think about what this pitcher threw me in the past in different situations. When the game starts I'll study the way the pitcher works other left-handed hitters ahead of me in the lineup.

Then I go to the plate and guess.

I don't know. I hear guys say, "I don't guess. I just see the ball and hit the ball."

I may have even said it myself a few times.

But I think for the most part you have to guess what's coming. If I sit on a fastball and the guy throws me a breaking ball, I have no chance of hitting it. The only way I can hit a breaking ball is if I'm looking for it. And over the last few years I think I've learned to do that, learned when to look for the breaking ball. For the most part, if a guy says he doesn't guess, he just reacts, I think he's lying, because there's just too short a time to react.

Ted Williams also said he could pick up the spin on the ball right out of the pitcher's hand, and maybe he could. He's got the numbers to back it up. Maybe Tony Gwynn and a couple other guys can do that. Not many, though.

Look at Ryne Sandberg. He's been a great hitter for a lot of years. Sometimes he looks foolish swinging at a pitch. Then you throw him the same pitch, same location, and he hits it off the wall or for a home run. So I have to believe the first time he guessed wrong but he swung anyway. And the second time he was sitting on it. That's the thing about being a good or a bad hitter: it's such a fine line. The difference between batting .200 and batting .300 is only one hit in ten at bats. One hit every two, two and a half games.

Pitchers make mistakes, and when they do, you'd damn well better hit it because if you don't, it just might be the last pitch you'll see to hit in that at bat. Somebody once told me that in every at bat you're going to get one pitch to hit, and when you get it you'd better hit it. That's how guys thrive.

There are a couple exceptions. Every scouting report I've ever seen on Barry Bonds says pitch him up and in, then down and away. Up and in, down and away. But I've seen him get that pitch down and away and hit a home run to left. And I've seen him get that pitch up and in and hit a home run to right. I've seen Tony Gwynn do the same thing without the power. They're good enough to hit the pitcher's pitch. But they're the exceptions.

Most guys better hit that mistake, because, if they don't, the pitcher is going to step back and say, "Man, I made a mistake and I got away with it. Now I'm really going after this guy."

If you get your pitch and don't hit it, you just have to bear down and try to put the ball in play. If you don't, the pitcher is going to bury you. And if the count gets to 0–2, forget it. If the count goes 0–2 too many times, that's when you find yourself back playing in the Sunday afternoon beer leagues.

So you guess. But it should be an educated guess.

You look at the stats they have these days. They break it down to how a guy hits against left-handers and right-handers, day and night, home and road, artificial turf and grass. I think you should toss all that and go with what you feel. It all comes down to hunches. Like, the Phillies platooned in left and right field last year. So, say Pete Incaviglia starts in left. He gets two hits. Now the other team brings in a right-handed relief pitcher. Do you take Incaviglia out and put Milt Thompson up to bat? Or do you stay with the guy who is hot? I say go with the guy who is swinging the bat well at that particular time. Otherwise it gets too complicated.

They put out these numbers every night. I don't know, sometimes you have nothing to do, so you read the reports. Sometimes they tell you the obvious, like with David Cone; I didn't mind seeing him go back to the American League. I've never hit him good, and I know it. But then there's a guy like Lee Smith. Now, according to the sheet of paper, I'm 0-for-14 against him or something like that. I've never gotten a hit off him. But I didn't know that until they told me. I was sure I had gotten a hit off him. There are other guys I can't remember ever getting a hit off, but according to the statistics, I've hit them pretty good. There's a big difference between what you feel and what the numbers show. I could have sworn I could hit Lee Smith, but then I saw those numbers and it started to get in my head. I think they should just throw those statistics out. If you went strictly by those reports, I'd never bat against Lee Smith.

We played a doubleheader against the Padres last year. The first game was rain-delayed. The second one started after midnight. Andy Benes, a right-hander, started the game, but Ricky Jordan started at first base. I went in to Jim Fregosi's office and I said, "Why aren't I playing? A right-handed pitcher, what the hell is going on?" But Fregosi had a hunch. And Ricky hit a three-run homer and we won the game.

I say hunch because I thought I had hit Benes pretty good. But Fregosi also knew that after Lenny Dykstra was in the car accident a couple years ago, Ricky played against the Padres and hit well. Then we went through an experimental stage where we weren't scoring runs, so Ricky played first and I was in the outfield, and I guess he hit Benes then, too. But if you go by how we had been doing things last year, I would have played against the right-hander. That's what I mean by a hunch.

Most platoons start right-handed hitters against left-handed pitchers and vice versa. That's the percentages. But it really depends more on how well you see the ball from a certain pitcher. There are some right-handers I hate to face, because I just can't pick the ball up as well. Last year there were some right-handers that gave Milt Thompson trouble, so Pete Inca-viglia would play even though we were facing a right-hander.

When I was in San Diego, if they decided to give Tony Gwynn a day off, it didn't matter how the guy pitched. If we were facing a young right-hander he didn't know and a nasty left-hander he'd seen a lot, he preferred to sit against the right-hander. He'd rather face the left-hander because he knew what he would throw him.

Usually you can get a pretty good idea of what a pitcher wants to do by watching the tapes and how he pitches to hitters similar to you. Most pitchers work right-handed hitters pretty much the same and left-handed hitters pretty much the same.

Say I'm watching a tape of a guy pitching against the Cubs. I'll watch what kind of pitches Mark Grace and Derrick May get. Maybe he'll fall into a pattern where he's starting them out with a first pitch breaking ball. So I'll go out there and sit on a first pitch breaking ball.

Now, sometimes a lot of good it does me because I can't hit it anyway. But at least I guessed right.

That's the only way you can do it. Pitchers are so good. They pretty much know what they're doing. If they throw a good breaking ball, it doesn't matter if you're looking for it or not, you're not going to hit it. If they throw a good fastball, no matter if you're looking for it or not, you're not going to hit it. That's why you have to live off mistakes.

I watch Lenny Dykstra his first at bat because he's left-handed and he hits before me. I watch the sequence of pitches he gets. It could be a little different than what I'll see because they know he takes the first pitch a lot of the time, so they might start him with a fastball. I'll take that into consideration. But is the pitcher going to throw Lenny breaking balls after that or is he going to keep throwing fastballs? I can get an idea of how he's working and factor that into my guessing pattern.

If the count gets to 2–0 and 3–1, you can pretty much look for your pitch. If he throws something else, let it go. But if he throws that pitch you're looking for and he throws it in the happy zone, you'd better hit it.

It's not just the pitchers you have to watch, either. It's the catcher, too. A lot of catchers will fall into a pattern. If they're ahead in the count, they'll call this pitch. Behind, that pitch. If you watch, you can really help yourself by learning a catcher's patterns.

For example, late in Gary Carter's career, if there was a guy on first who could run, you could guarantee a fastball. Say I'm at bat and Lenny Dykstra is on first. I'm looking for a fastball every pitch, because Carter didn't want anyone stealing a base off him. He thought it was degrading. He didn't want people to say, "Well, you know, his arm isn't as good as it used to be." It was a pride thing, and you can feed off pride. Carter had been a great throwing catcher and even when he didn't throw as well he still had that pride. You can use that to your advantage.

Some catchers will call a first pitch breaking ball, second pitch fastball, third pitch breaking ball, no matter what the count is. If they do that, by your second or third at bat you should have a pretty good idea what's coming. Last year we picked up on that more than we ever had because each game was so important. As the game went on, we talked a lot among ourselves on the bench. Or Lenny, even if he made an out, would walk past me in the on-deck circle, and he'd say, "Did you see that his breaking ball was going sharply down?" or

"He's throwing more of a hard slider." Or whatever. And that would help when I went up.

You can tell little things from on deck or from the bench, but you're not always sure. It's up to the guys batting ahead of you to help you. And Lenny was real good at that.

The thing is, even if you've faced a pitcher before, he's not going to be exactly the same pitcher every time. Say we played Montreal early in the year and Dennis Martinez started. At that point in the season, he might be throwing 90 miles an hour. Then, later in the year, he's a little tired and he's not throwing quite as hard. We'll talk about that. Because if you gear up for a 90-mile-an-hour fastball and it comes in at 85 or 86, you're not going to hit it.

The difference between pitchers as the year goes on can be significant. As they build up innings, build up pitch counts, they wear down a little, and you can gear yourself for that. It makes the guessing game a little easier because you have just a little more time to adjust to what he's throwing.

Sometimes they can fool you, though. Look at a guy like Rick Reuschel. He didn't throw hard, especially later in his career with the Giants. If you noticed, if he got into a situation early where he had runners in scoring position, he'd throw sinker away, sinker away, sinker away, and hope to get a ground ball. But later in the game, if he got in the same situation, he could hump up and throw it harder.

Dwight Gooden can do the same thing. I don't know if he saves himself or what, but if he has a couple men on base it seems like he'll throw five miles an hour harder than he did your first at bat. And that makes it tough. That's the learning process. Gooden probably realizes he doesn't have the same fastball he had when he was a rookie and during his first couple years. He can still blow people away, but now he just waits for the right opportunity to do it.

When Gooden first came up, he was unbelievable. With just

a few guys—Nolan Ryan, Goose Gossage, guys like that—it didn't matter if you knew what was coming. They could tell you straight out, "Here comes a fastball," and it would still be tough. I had some success against Dwight early on, but whenever I got a hit I always wondered how I'd done it.

As the years went on and he developed a good breaking ball, I had more trouble with him. He knows that when he pitches, I'm geared for the hard one. When he throws the breaking ball, I'm not going to hit it. He knows it. I know it. And we go from there. All I know is that if he does throw me a fastball I'd better hit it, because if I don't and he keeps throwing breaking balls, I'm done.

Like I said, hitting ain't easy. I don't think pitchers realize that even if they don't have their best stuff, it's still hard to hit. Pitchers sometimes also don't realize how hard they throw. Take Tommy Greene. He thinks he's throwing 60 miles an hour and has to nibble. He just doesn't realize.

The thing that really bothers me is when a pitcher throws at a batter. It hurts to get hit by a pitch. I can't think of anyone who enjoys getting hit, except maybe Tim Flannery when I was in San Diego and Dave Hollins with the Phillies now.

To me, it's not worth taking a chance that the pitch could crack your elbow or mess up your knee. So I always try to get out of the way.

Dave Hollins doesn't move. He seems to enjoy it. He seems to get a kick out of it in a masochistic sort of way. And the only time he ever went after a pitcher was when Bob Scanlan threw one at his head while we were playing the Cubs late in the 1992 season.

You want to give people enough credit to say they would never intentionally throw at someone's head. You've got to give them the benefit of the doubt, because no matter how big an idiot you are, to throw at someone's head is to take a chance of killing or permanently injuring him. I think you have to give pitchers, and people in general, more credit than that.

Look at Dickie Thon. He was on his way to being one of the best shortstops the National League has ever seen. Then he got hit in the face with a pitch. I'm not saying it was done on purpose. I have no idea. But it can happen. You can basically end a guy's career.

When the other team is throwing at your hitters, you expect your pitchers to protect you. That's why the fight we had with the Cardinals in St. Petersburg last spring was so important.

It all started in the first inning. Donovan Osborne, their pitcher, hit Dave Hollins with a pitch. Osborne came to bat in the third. Our pitcher, Tommy Greene, hit him.

That could have been the end of it. But when Greene came to bat in the fifth, Tom Urbani knocked him off the plate with four pitches.

Another Cardinals pitcher, Paul Kilgus, hit Wes Chamberlain with a pitch in the sixth. In the seventh, Mariano Duncan homered. Two pitches later, Kilgus hit Ricky Jordan. That's when the benches emptied.

The year before, we led the league in being hit by pitches. In this game with the Cardinals, Dave Hollins was hit on the top of the shoulder with an 0–2 pitch. It was like, "Do we let this continue, or do we do something about it?" So we did something. It just got a little out of hand.

When a player gets hit, the pitcher always says he was just trying to pitch inside, but sometimes you have to wonder. So there are two ways to handle it. If you get hit and you think it was an accident and it's below the shoulders, you can just take your base and let your pitcher take care of it. But sometimes you have to make the point that you're not going to take it anymore. Osborne hit Dave; Tommy Greene hit Osborne. Okay, we're even. But apparently we weren't. No one is ever going to admit it, but it sure seemed funny to me that a guy like Paul Kilgus with pinpoint control is all of a sudden throwing the ball *behind* the batter.

But I think that was a big day because we let people know

we weren't going to take it anymore. And it showed us something, too, because we didn't think most of our pitchers had the balls to protect us. We knew Terry Mulholland would, but we weren't real sure about the others.

Pitchers have to throw inside. I understand that. Knock us off the plate. Fine. Maybe they even have to hit people from time to time. But do it below the shoulders. If you're throwing that hard and you're throwing at someone's head, you could kill them or blind them. Something that doesn't have to do with baseball but with the rest of their lives and their ability to function normally.

That's scary. It's one of the hazards of the job. Boys will be boys and that's fine and dandy. But throwing at somebody's head isn't. Hitting is hard enough without that.

Time for the chick to leave the nest.

I WAS TWENTY-FIVE YEARS OLD WHEN I
made it to the Padres in 1986. Single. Playing baseball. Living in San Diego. Making $60,000. That was the major league minimum, but I thought if they'd sign me to a three-year contract for $60,000 a year, I could retire.

It didn't suck.

But I was also a little intimidated by everything that first year. I didn't adapt well—again. I didn't know what to expect. I was living in a city, a big city, for the first time. Just about everybody else on the team was married, so I was living by myself, basically for the first time. I didn't know what the hell to do. I couldn't cook. I couldn't do laundry. All my shirts were basically the same color because they all got thrown into the same wash.

The first day there, Tim Flannery helped me find a great place to live. There was a guy who had played in the minor leagues for the Pirates for a long time, Steve Smith. He was a minor league manager and I rented his house. It was only about a mile or two from Flannery's. We had the day off with a workout in the evening, so Flannery came and got me and showed me all around. He showed me where everything was. It was really thoughtful of him to do that for me.

Of course, by the time we pulled back into the driveway I had forgotten everything.

So after the workout, he asked me if I could find my way home. I said, "Yeah." He asked if I was sure. I said, "Yeah, I'll find it."

Well, the next thing I remember is seeing a sign that said it was ten miles to Los Angeles. I thought, "Man, this seems a lot farther than it was before." But I kept driving. I was so lost I ended up everywhere. It took me four hours to get home.

It was different being a rookie then. I think it all goes back to the minor league thing. Back then you really had to work hard to get to the big leagues. Now it's like, if you have two bad years and then one decent year, all of a sudden you're the greatest thing since sliced bread. You can't miss. Anyway, the Padres weren't good at building up their minor league players. You had no fanfare coming in. It's not like the Phillies have been with Tyler Green and some other guys, where everbody says, "This guy can't miss. Can't wait till he gets here. He's going to be in the big leagues in a year or two."

Back then, if you played three years in the minor leagues that was a short time. It was usually four or five. And nobody knew who you were. Nobody spoke to me or Tony Gwynn or Kevin McReynolds. Maybe Flannery, but that's about it.

Most of them just went their own way and treated a rookie like a rookie. Until you've done something, until you've helped us, fuck you. Maybe it's not so good now, the way they build up minor leaguers. They might be a little more fragile. Me? I just thought that's the way it was supposed to be.

I sat in the front of the plane on road trips. I figured that's where I should sit. I didn't say a thing. I never even thought about going to the back of the plane, because that's where the veterans were. I was just a little piece of shit and I would sit where they told me to sit. Then one day on a bus to the airport, Goose Gossage asked me if I liked country music. I told him I did. He said, "Why don't you come to the back of the bus with us, then? We listen to country music back here." And I've been back there ever since.

The young guys today, they're built up so much that when they get to the majors they feel like they deserve to be there. It wasn't until my fifth or sixth year that I felt like I belonged. Now they're here one day and you see them playing their own music, ordering the clubhouse kids around: "Go get me a cup of coffee, go get me this, go get me that." What the hell is that? When I broke in, I was the guy being ordered around. I poured more coffee that first year than the International House of Pancakes. If the veterans wanted coffee, I went and got it. There was nothing else I could do.

It made me appreciate being in the majors and it made me work harder. There are too many guys now who come up and just because they got here, they think that's it; they quit doing what they did to get here in the first place. So I don't agree with some people who have said that some of the Phillies veterans aren't nice enough to the young players who come up. Hell, they had it easier than I did when I came up. But I guess that's just the way it is today.

Jim Fregosi lets us police the players, right? But when Kevin Stocker came up, we also knew we needed a shortstop. So Fregosi called a bunch of us in. And he said, "Be kind to him." And we said, "We already are. We put him down at our end of the clubhouse."

He said, "Oh, shit."

But we let Stocker come down to our end because we knew how vital he was to our team. We didn't want to put him down next to the pitchers. They have a different perspective of the game. They can screw you up. So we wanted him down close to where we were.

We were easy on Stocker. We haven't been accused of being easy on young players often. We got on him a little bit and he took it and accepted it, but for the most part we were gentle. We left him alone because he could play. If you can't play and you come in talking trash, you're going to get buried.

Stocker never said much. He just proved to us he knew how to play the game. He didn't try to tell us he knew, he just showed us. And two months after he got there, we didn't look at him as a rookie; he was a professional. Of course, if he had come in and talked trash and backed it up, that would have been fine, too.

Goose Gossage was good to me when I went to the Padres. He'd invite me over to his house to eat all the time. One time we had an off-day. He had rented a place on the beach, a big old beach house, and we were having a team party out there. It didn't start until one in the afternoon, but he called me about ten. He said, "Come on, you ain't married, you're coming with me."

We drove around and picked up some stuff. It was the first

time we had really just talked. He told me about how when he was growing up he had to sleep in the same bed with his mother and two sisters until he was drafted. That's how poor they were. You have to respect somebody who goes through something like that. I just think he's a great guy.

I don't think people knew him the way they should have, because he wouldn't let them. My first encounter with him was my first spring training with the Padres. If I didn't make weight, they were going to send me home. I had to maintain a certain weight for the whole spring training, and my exercise program was on a stationary bike.

Well, Goose didn't run with the pitchers. He'd come in in the morning and ride the bike. So the first time I met him I was riding the bike. I was about halfway through my program when he walked in and said, "That's my bike." And I said, "Yes, sir," and I got off and walked out of the trainers' room.

He came out and said, "Hey, come here."

I said, "What?"

He said, "There's sweat on this bike. Wipe it off."

I said, "Okay."

A lot of rookies now would just refuse to get off. Wouldn't matter if you were a veteran or what. But I think in a simple way I earned his respect, and after that, we never had a problem. I knew when he was coming in and when I could get on the bike and finish my program, which was before he got there. So I had to get in earlier. If Goose Gossage says to come in earlier and get done before he gets there, you do it. Hey, I'm not stupid. I watch games. I'd seen him pitch in the World Series. I'd seen how dominant he was coming out of the bullpen. The man deserved my respect.

Flannery helped me out a lot, too. We'd go to a place called Charlie's, right near where we lived. We got to meet the guy who ran the place. They were nice to me. The next few years, I pretty much had my own stool in the place.

He also tried to get me interested in surfing. Of course, he told me I'd need a two-car garage door and a leash to do it; he said that was the only thing that would hold me up.

The big leagues were different. When you play in the minor leagues, you don't think about what the other teams in your division are doing. You don't even think they've got a game. You think you're the only ones. That changes when you come up.

The year before, the front office had told me I was going to get called up in September, but when the time came, I wasn't one of the ones they brought up. I was really pissed off. I got an attitude. "Fuck them. I'm quitting."

But then what?

I went home and everybody was asking me, "What are you going to do?" And I said, "I guess I'm going back."

Guys get mad at the organization all the time and say they're going to quit. Well, who cares? You think the game is going to miss you? If you're Michael Jordan and you decide not to play anymore, they're going to miss you. But if you're in the minor leagues and you quit, who gives a shit? You think Abner Doubleday is going to roll over in his grave? Hell, no.

But now I had finally made it and I have to admit, it was pretty exciting. I still remember the first time I was ever on a big league field. We were playing an exhibition game against San Diego State at Jack Murphy Stadium and I thought it was the most awesome thing in the world.

Everybody else was, you know, "Cripes, we have to play an exhibition. What a joke. Oh, man, we have to play these guys. What is this? If we lose we're gonna get ragged. Somebody could get hurt."

And I was there, all dressed and ready to go. "I'll play. I'll play."

Then we went up to Los Angeles to open the season and I made my infamous first appearance in the big leagues.

It was as a pinch-runner. Who'd have thunk it? Carmelo Martinez was hitting and they put me in to pinch-run. They told me it was going to be a hit-and-run. There were runners on first and third and they told me before I went out there that they were going to put the play on because they wanted to get the run in. They wanted to stay out of the double play because Carmelo didn't run that well. But they also said, "Don't get picked off. You're not stealing a base, so whatever you do, don't get picked off."

Fernando Valenzuela was pitching and they kept telling me what a great pickoff move he had and to be sure he released the ball before I broke to second. So I did. Now I'm running down to second base and Carmelo takes the pitch right down the middle for a strike. And like you're supposed to do, I peeked and looked back and saw what happened.

I said, "Oh-oh."

Second base looked like it was a five-dollar cab ride away. Mike Scioscia, the Dodgers catcher, threw the ball. So I stopped. I figured I'd get in a rundown, that it was my only chance. Well, Scioscia threw the ball high and Steve Sax, the second baseman, had to jump for it.

Later they tried to say that if I had kept running I'd have been safe. Let me tell you, he could have jumped, come down, and probably thrown it around the infield and still tagged me by the time I got there, that's how far away I was. So I got in the rundown and I got tagged out and the run didn't score.

That was my first real experience with the media. After the game the reporters came right to my locker. They said, "You lost the game." And I was like, "What did I do? Did I give up six runs? No."

After that base-running adventure I was used as a pinch-hitter the next night and I flied out. Then we went somewhere else. I got a couple more at bats as a pinch-hitter. I think I was 0-for-3.

Now, if you go a week into the season and you don't have a hit, it doesn't matter if you're 0-for-1 or 0-for-24. I was thinking I'd never get a hit.

But I got my first major league hit in the home opener in San Diego. It was the bottom of the ninth and we were losing by a run. I guess we had run out of pinch-hitters or something. Bob Welch started and was still pitching for the Dodgers. I had a 3–2 count and fouled off a couple pitches. And then I got a hit to right field.

They all said I couldn't pull the ball. I guess I showed them.

Actually, it was a seeing-eye hit. It was on the ground, anyway. I didn't hit it bad. It was between Sax and Greg Brock. That shows you how old I am. Greg Brock was still playing then.

The tying run scored. I was excited. Everybody was standing up and clapping because we had tied the game. Then they flashed on the scoreboard it was my first major league hit. You know how home openers are. Even in San Diego they aren't bad. Everybody was cheering and all I could think was, "Oh, my God. I did something good."

Then the next thought was, "I hope they don't put me in for defense."

But they didn't, and Bruce Bochy hit a home run to win the game for us a couple innings later. It was pretty neat.

I was used mostly as a pinch-hitter my rookie year and batted .309. We had a disappointing season, lost eighty-eight games. Some of the crowds weren't that big, but I never really gave it a thought. If I'd been a little older, if I had played a few years, I might have been disappointed. I don't know. I was just glad to be there.

The next year was worse. We lost ninety-seven games and finished last. Larry Bowa had replaced Steve Boros as manager. He didn't make a real smooth transition. He was just being himself. And, to be honest, it probably wasn't the ideal place for his first time to be a manager in the big leagues.

He cared so much. And the people in San Diego, the ones who came to the games then, they loved the team. They loved the players. But San Diego is so laid-back. You can go in anywhere, any place near the stadium after a game, and they'll come up to you. But it's not like Philly, where you feel like you're in a trash compactor, because they just squeeze you. It's a whole different thing.

San Diegans are polite people. They come up and ask you how you're doing. You did good last night, sorry about the game, nice talking to you and that's it. It's never, "What's wrong with this guy? What's wrong with the team?" I've been in places where they're asking what the hell's wrong with Mitch, what the hell is wrong with you, what's Darren Daulton doing out there? In Philadelphia, it's *win*. There it was, oh, well, we'll get them tomorrow.

In Philly, people come to the games because they want to be there. They live for it. In San Diego, there's so much else to do. It's like, "It's six-thirty. What do you want to do? How about we go watch the Padres?" It's almost like an accident that they come to the games. That's just the way people are there. It's more like a social thing than a live-or-die thing—which is probably good. I have a lot of respect for players who broke in with Philadelphia; I got to play a few years in San Diego before I graduated to becoming an asshole.

Still, as I said before, that was the year I got my first chance to play every day. Steve Garvey got hurt and Bowa played me. I batted .313. That was great. But I had played on some good teams in the minors. I was happy to be in the big leagues, and I was happy to be making a lot of money, but there's nothing like winning. Money can't buy that, and it just didn't happen. It never got to the point where it was hard for us to go to the ballpark, but it was a situation where we came in wondering how we were going to lose that night instead of thinking about how we were going to win. You could sense that in a lot of players.

Bowa was fired in May 1988, and that's when things started to go wrong for me in San Diego. When he was the manager, I knew coming to the ballpark that I was playing. I knew who was pitching, and from what I'd watched and what I'd learned, I tried to remember what he throws. I talked to people. I came to the ballpark prepared, and when I came in and got dressed I did what I had to do.

With Bowa gone, I could only hope I'd be playing that day. I know I wasn't playing good. I hurt my shoulder. But in my mind it all went back to platooning again. I'd start playing good, and then I'd sit. Then I'd be back in the lineup feeling like I had to get seven hits in five at bats to be sure of playing again the next day.

They always said I had trouble hitting left-handers. I don't know, I was hitting them when I was playing everyday. You're doing something, you're having success, then all of a sudden the person who was with you is gone. Like a boxer who wins the heavyweight title, then his trainer or manager leaves, and he's a totally different person.

The man who was in my corner, who stood by me when the front office said not to play me every day, was gone. And I'm thinking, "Oh, shit, what's going to happen now?"

I thought I had a good year the year before. I thought I was doing okay up until that point. I figured Jack McKeon had to keep playing me. But after a few games when I guess maybe I didn't do so well, all of a sudden I was platooning. The next spring they wanted me to play right field because they'd gotten Jack Clark, so I went and played right field. But it just wasn't comfortable.

And that wasn't all.

A couple friends from back home, guys I had grown up with, had come to San Diego to visit me a few times my second year. During the winter we rented a place out there. I was gone to winter ball most of the time. The next year we lived together, all three of us. They were good friends and we had some good times. Sometimes, while I was on the road, they'd drive back home to West Virginia.

One day I was sitting in the clubhouse and two guys came over to my locker. They said they wanted to talk to me. I told them to sit down. They said they'd rather go somewhere else.

I said, "Nah, sit down, this is where I talk to everybody."

One guy pulled out his wallet and identified himself as an FBI agent. He said, "Please, come with us."

I went with them.

It turned out that my friends had robbed some banks. They hadn't been caught yet and the FBI had been trailing me, hoping that I would lead them to my friends, but I hadn't seen them in a while.

It was scary. I mean, that somebody could follow me like that and I wouldn't even know it. I wasn't sure I believed it until one of the FBI agents said, "You know that girl you were talking to the other night? She wasn't so hot. And, by the way, you really should be more careful about driving home after you've had a couple beers."

That made a believer out of me.

I didn't know what was going to happen. Rumors started going around that someone had told my friends I was the one who had called the FBI on them. I was really shaky about the whole thing. Baseball was not really high on my list of priorities right then.

It got to the point where after games I'd have to go and call the FBI and report to them if I'd seen my friends or not. It was a tense situation. They caught one of the guys early in the summer. They didn't catch the other one until September. I heard later that he was about a mile from where I lived and that he had a gun when they caught him.

Looking back on it now, I understand what happened and

why they did what they did. I have no animosity whatsoever
and, when they get out of jail, we'll probably hang out again.
The guy with the gun called me when I got home that October.
He said he made a mistake and he apologized and he hoped he
hadn't ruined my career.

He said he knew it had to affect the way I'd played. I said,
"Hey, don't worry about it. It's over now. The only thing that
matters is to get better, get your health, do your time, and
come out and be the person we know." I've got to believe he's
still a good person, regardless. Everyone makes mistakes. I've
made a couple myself.

I ended up hitting .241 that year, but there was no excuse
for playing as bad as I played.

I think that experience made me a little more careful about
the things I do. I was in shock to hear that my friends had been
robbing banks and that the FBI was following me most of the
summer. I thought about that when Ed Rendell, the mayor of
Philadelphia, said the death threats to Mitch Williams were
nothing to worry about. If somebody could follow me around
for a whole summer, why couldn't somebody follow Mitch for
one day if they really wanted to do something to him? It made
me leery of everything. There were nights I'd drive home after
they told me that, and if I thought somebody was following
me, I'd go out of my way to try to lose them.

One night after a game at Jack Murphy Stadium I couldn't
lose the car behind me. I was driving around and every time I
turned, the car behind me took the same turn. Finally I said to
hell with it. I knew some people were mad at me because I was
playing so bad. I could hear people yelling at me from the
stands. I had never experienced that before, except in Mexico
—and I couldn't understand what they were yelling at me back
then.

Anyway, after a while I figured maybe it was somebody I
knew and they were just trying to mess with me. So I pulled

onto the street where I lived and I stopped the car. I got out and I went back and I said, "What the hell do you want?"

They said they just wanted to tell me they thought I sucked. And then they drove off.

Now what kind of life is that? Following me around for an hour and a half just to tell me I suck. Hell, I know I sucked that year. Could have saved them a lot of time.

The following June I was traded to the Phillies. I didn't care by then; if there had been a team on the moon, they could have sent me there. I just had to go somewhere else. It was time to go.

I was glad to get out. I thought management treated us like kids. I didn't like that they didn't let us have beer in the clubhouse. I didn't like the way I was being used. You had to have a career game or the next day you were a no-show. I wasn't playing good. I was batting .184 when I was traded. I say I didn't get along with Jack McKeon, but the one thing he did do for me was to trade me. He could have kept me sitting around on the bench for the rest of the year. Then I would have had two full years of being horseshit, and who knows what would have happened after that? He gave me an opportunity to go somewhere else, and I'll always appreciate that.

I'll always be grateful to the Padres for drafting me. San Diego was beautiful. Who wouldn't want to live there? Beach, mountains, whatever you want is right there. It just got to the point that it was time to go.

You hear people talk about free agents. People wonder how they could leave after an organization has taken such good care of them. What they don't realize is that we only play baseball part of the time. The rest of the time we have to live. We have a life. Nothing against the city; San Diego was good to me. But it was time. Time for the chick to leave the nest.

If you screw up, the Philadelphia fans are going to know you screwed up. And they're going to boo you. Personally, I like that. It makes it easier to concentrate.

MY CAREER IN PHILADELPHIA DIDN'T GET

off to a wonderful start.

I was playing every day and getting a few hits. It was nice to come to the ballpark again and know I was going to be in the lineup. I was still bothered by the way nobody on the team seemed to give a shit, but I was trying not to let that get to me.

And then, in my fifth game for the Phillies, it happened.

We were playing the Pirates at Veterans Stadium. Pittsburgh was in fifth place. We were last. There weren't many people at the game.

The Phillies were ahead, 3–0, going into the fourth inning. Ken Howell was pitching. Barry Bonds was leading off for the Pirates in those days. Ken Howell had faced nine batters through the first three innings. The only batter who had reached base was Bobby Bonilla in the second, and he was thrown out trying to steal.

But Bonds homered to start off the fourth inning. Jose Lind singled. Andy Van Slyke grounded out. Lind went to second on the play, ran to third on a wild pitch, and scored when Bonilla doubled.

The next batter was R. J. Reynolds. He hit a fly ball to left, an easy play. I made the catch, put my head down, and started jogging back to the infield.

There was just one problem.

That was only the second out.

Bonilla tagged up and scored the tying run all the way from second on the sacrifice fly.

I got booed pretty good. See, I told you the Philly fans were knowledgeable.

That wasn't much fun. Something like that is really stupid. You can understand physical mistakes: striking out, making an error. Those things you can handle. But when you do something stupid, you can't handle that. It's something you wouldn't wish on anyone.

I remember saying to myself, "Everybody is thinking, 'God, what is it with this guy? We got him and he's hitting .180. And now he's dumber than hell, too.' " You know, if you're hitting .180 you'd better be damn intelligent. You'd better move all the runners and make all the plays. And you'd damn sure better remember how many outs there are.

When the media asked me about it after the game, I told them the truth. "I just had a brain fart."

I thought that was about the lowest I could get.

I was wrong, of course. You know the old baseball saying about how it's amazing that the guy who makes the great play in the field always seems to lead off the next inning? Sure enough, I was first up against John Smiley.

He struck me out on three pitches.

Then they really started booing. Welcome to Philadelphia. I could see these fans had come by their reputation honestly.

I can make light of it now because we came back and won the game. I had a couple hits in my last two at bats, and that helped. If we hadn't won, I don't know what would have happened. I was figuring this could be a long tenure—or, more truthfully, it was going to seem long even if I was only with the Phillies for a short time.

Fortunately things started getting better after that.

When I was first traded, a lot of people assumed I would be unhappy. Like I said, San Diego is a beautiful place to live. The Phillies were in last place. And Philadelphia has this reputation of being a tough town to play in.

But getting traded was the best thing that ever happened to me. I was back closer to home. It probably just goes to show how screwed up I am, but I felt a lot more comfortable playing in Philadelphia than I had in San Diego.

One thing is that I've always enjoyed hitting in Veterans Stadium. I was looking foward to playing all those home games there.

And it was a big change going from we'll-get-them-tomorrow to you-bastards-better-win-tonight. I don't know, there's something wrong with getting cheered when you make an out just because you ran hard to first. That's your job, you know? It just didn't make sense to me that the people in San Diego would cheer for that. In Philly, you can hit a ball into the hole, and the shortstop makes a great play and you dive in headfirst, but it doesn't matter because you weren't safe. "Boooo."

If you screw up, the Philadelphia fans are going to know you screwed up. And they're going to boo you. Personally, I like that. It makes it easier to concentrate.

Maybe I'm different, but I think the fans' reaction makes me play better. Because we've all got egos, and no matter what anybody tries to tell you, we don't like getting booed. In San Diego it's easier just to take your mistakes in stride: "Oh, I made another out." And I think that's what got me out of there, the fact that I couldn't take them in stride. If I made an out, I felt like I'd failed, no matter whether I'd lined out or what. In San Diego they accepted failure. In Philadelphia they don't accept it.

One thing that makes Philly different is what happened in 1964. The Phillies had a six-and-a-half-game lead with twelve games left to play and didn't win the pennant. We found out last year that the people still haven't forgotten that.

As players, we didn't pay the 1964 disaster any mind. There were only a few of us who were even born then, and not many of us are such great baseball historians that we would know or remember that.

But it kept coming up every day in the papers somewhere. Even when we went to Montreal in September somebody held up a sign, "Remember 1964." But I don't think we really worried about it. It's not like we played with any of them. We didn't know much about that season. But I know a lot of people were talking about it.

I don't want to say the fans of Philadelphia were expecting us to lose. But I think in the back of their minds they thought there was a chance we wouldn't win the division, and they didn't want to be disappointed.

It takes a certain type of player to play his best in certain cities. There are some guys, they may be great players, but they might just not be suited to playing in a certain place.

Take New York. Lenny Dykstra loved playing for the Mets. He still loves going back to Shea Stadium and playing. That's why I think a general manager someplace like New York or Philadelphia should take a guy's personality into account before he makes a trade.

I feel comfortable in Philadelphia, but I wouldn't in New York. And a lot of guys feel that way. I remember talking to Kevin McReynolds one day during the 1986 season. I don't know how the subject came up, but he told me, "If I ever get traded to New York, I'll quit. I'll never play another game."

That December I was watching ESPN one night. I was playing in Mexico but living in the United States. So I'm watching TV and they come on and they say, "Padres trade outfielder to Mets."

I was thinking, "Oh, man, don't tell me. I've gotta go to New York." There had been some rumors that I might be traded. And then they flashed up a picture. It was McReynolds, not me.

I called him right up. He said, "I don't want to hear it. I just don't want to hear it. Just shut up."

I said, "Are you quittin'?"

He said, "Shut up."

I said, "If you're going to retire, I'll give you some money. I'll help you out."

He said, "Fuck you. I'm going. Just shut up."

I said, "Man, you're crazy. I don't know if I could play there."

You know, though, after Kevin got settled in, I think he enjoyed it all right. And now he's back in New York. Amazing. Some guys really take to it after they get there. I think there might be a few too many people for me, though. And it gives me a lot of respect for a guy like Dwight Gooden, who's played his whole career there. That ain't an easy place to play. Of course, when you're that good, it's probably a little easier.

That's one thing about the fans in Philadelphia. You always hear that they're negative, that they boo all the time. Well, like I said, that doesn't bother me. But the other part that nobody seems to talk about is the way they get behind a team that plays hard and wins.

When I first came to Philly, we got booed a lot more than we did a couple years later, even though we were still in last place. And I think the reason is that, by then, even though we weren't winning as much as we wanted to, we went out and busted our ass every night. Philly fans appreciate that.

You just have to look at the way they supported us last year, not just by coming out to the games but by really cheering when we did something right or when we needed a rally in the ninth inning.

The thing about baseball is that the season is so long. There are so many games that there are going to be times when you struggle. I don't care how great a player you are. Look at Barry Bonds: he had one of the best seasons anybody has had in years, but he still went through a period when he struggled. There's no way physically or mentally you can be at your best for 162 games.

You don't think about it. You don't even realize it. You just know you're in a slump, and then maybe you go back and watch a bunch of videotape. Then you start messing around with your stance. It gets to be too much stress on your brain. You're up there telling yourself your feet should be here and your hands should be there. And all the while there's a guy out there throwing 90 miles an hour and while you're telling yourself all this stuff, the count gets to 0–2. And then you're really screwed.

When you're going through something like that, I think it helps to hear something from the fans. Even boos. And I found out right away that Philly fans knew how to do that.

Sometimes you wake up in the morning and you're in that early morning fog. And you wonder where the hell you are, because all the hotel rooms look the same.

ONE TIME I WAS GOING TO A GAME IN A

cab with Steve Garvey. He asked me if I had seen some monument, then he asked me if I'd been to a certain museum. I told him that I hadn't. He said I needed to get out more. I told him I really wasn't interested.

He didn't understand that. I guess a lot of people don't.

They think we go to all these beautiful cities, we stay in the best hotels, we have the money to eat in the finest restaurants. And it's all true.

Somebody asks me what a certain city is like and, really, all I can usually tell them is whether the ballpark is good or shitty and what the room service is like. I'm the one everyone on the team asks about room service, because that's usually what I eat.

See, I'm not into sight-seeing. Even on an off-day, I never really take the time to go out and see the cities we play in. I go there to do a job, and that's to play baseball.

I've never even seen the Liberty Bell.

I did see the big Phillies hat they put on the statue of William Penn on top of City Hall. But of course I saw it on television.

Garvey was trying to tell me about all the architectural designs on all these buildings, why they're so beautiful. But architecture means nothing to me. I want somebody to build a nice house for me someday; they might build a terrible one, but I wouldn't know. I mean, I'd know in a few years if it started falling apart, but that would be it. Steve wanted me to go to art museums. Well, I don't want to go look at a bunch of paintings when I don't know what the hell they are. So I just don't go.

Here's another thing. Say I get back to the hotel after a night game at one or two o'clock in the morning. I like to be at the park at noon or one for a game the next night. That doesn't leave time for much more than a quick sleep.

To make the picture complete, I really don't like to fly. So life on the road isn't one of my favorite things.

That doesn't mean that all cities are exactly alike.

I'm not real fond of San Francisco. I know it's supposed to be a great city, and in some ways it probably is. But the ballpark is a hellhole. It's just miserable. The guys who have to play there all the time say it's not that bad when you get used to it. I don't know if I believe them. I can see how you might get used to playing in a run-down old stadium. You could get used to that. But I don't see how you could get used to the paper and dirt and trash all flying around and into your eyes. Miserable. It's not human.

I have to say, when it looked like they were going to move the Giants to Florida, I wasn't upset. Another trip to Florida, where it's warm, would have been fine with me. But somebody came up with the right price and kept them in San Francisco. You can bet the guy who came up with the money never played there. He never had to try to play with all that wind.

I think they should let the players make more decisions, but I guess they think we're all idiots. They pay us the money and we should just be quiet and do as we're told.

I've always had trouble picking up the ball in San Francisco and Los Angeles. Especially San Francisco, now that they've put those new seats in left field at Candlestick Park. I talked to Will Clark about it one day down at first base. I said, "You can't pick the ball up here in the daytime."

He said, "Tell me about it. It's terrible."

Of course, then you look at Barry Bonds and he's hitting about six thousand home runs, and you think if you hold him to a single you've done a helluva job. So he wasn't having too much trouble.

It's the same way in San Diego. It was, even when I played there. The backdrop isn't really straight, and when you're batting against a tall right-handed pitcher like Andy Benes, you can't really see, because when he releases the ball it's coming right out of the people who are sitting out there.

When I was playing there, I complained about it. I told someone on the grounds crew. I asked if there was any way they could move the backdrop or put a bigger tarp out there so we could see. Well, he told the general manager. And the GM made the worst possible mistake: he said, "Let's ask Tony

Gwynn." Hell, Tony could hit .300 in the dark. So they asked the wrong guy and the backdrop still hasn't been changed.

I don't like New York. It's like a whole city full of little Lennys running around, running here, running there, can't sit still. I think that's why he fit in there and why they want him back. Too bad. We're not giving him back. We're keeping him.

But those people are on the go, nonstop, twenty-four hours a day. You get back to the hotel at two o'clock in the morning and there are people waiting out front for autographs. You try to get into a cab or go to a restaurant to eat and they swarm around you. And they're impatient. You're half done signing and they're off. I've had guys run up the street, sticking stuff in the windows for you to sign while your cab is moving. Where I come from, it may take a person ten minutes to walk twenty feet. It's a lot slower.

I do enjoy playing in New York, though. The fans are like Philly fans, real knowledgeable. They know what's going on. And they've got some great hecklers. Some of those guys, they talk with that Noo Yawk accent and I get a kick out of it.

Say it's right before game time. Now, you know New York fans aren't going to *ask* you to sign their baseball or their card. It's "Hey, sign dis." And if you don't, it's "You asshole. You jerkoff." It's funny. Just listening to them is pretty neat.

I like Atlanta. It's fun. It used to be bad when there were two thousand people at the games; that was dull. But now they have sellouts all the time.

I like playing in St. Louis, too. It seems like the people in the Midwest know the game and they come out and support their teams. St. Louis, Cincinnati, Chicago—those are three of my favorite places to play. Chicago for Wrigley Field. Cincinnati because I always liked the Reds. St. Louis because it always seems so clean.

Those are probably my three favorites. Once you get East and West of there it gets a little shaky.

But I also don't think I could play at any of those places as a home player. St. Louis is way too hot. Chicago has too many day games. Cincinnati might be the only place I'd have a chance.

I don't like Olympic Stadium in Montreal. It's dark in there, like playing in a dungeon.

But eventually we always end up going back to the hotel. People walk through the lobby and they see the fancy furniture and the big chandeliers, and they think it must really be neat to stay there. But a room is a room. It's got a bed and a desk and a TV. That's all I need, but what's so fantastic about that? I've got that at home. I don't have a chandelier and I don't have cable TV, but I have a satellite dish that gets a lot more channels.

I really don't go out much; I stay in my room a lot more than I used to. One reason is that I just don't rebound as quickly as I used to. And another reason is that going out can be a hassle.

Every once in a while I'll go down to the hotel bar and have a drink, but that's not always a lot of fun. You might be in a slump, or you might be thinking about the game tomorrow, and people want to come up and buy you a drink and talk. You feel bad if you tell them no, but sometimes you just don't feel like it.

It's a trade-off: it's not a lot of fun to go back to your room by yourself with the door locked and the phone blocked, but sometimes it's better than going downstairs where some stranger wants to be your best friend for a couple hours.

Some glamorous life.

I've seen the stories about some of the problems Charles Barkley has had in bars on the road. I got to know him when he played for the 76ers, and he's a great guy. A helluva guy. He says he's not going to let people force him to stay in his room. More power to him. But it's got to be a headache.

That's his individual feeling. He's comfortable in crowds. Personally, I'm not. I hate feeling crowded. If I'm sitting at a table in a restaurant or I'm sitting in a bar and it gets crowded, I feel like the walls are closing in and that my head is going to explode.

And look at the two of us. I'm five feet ten and two hundred pounds, or a little more. He's what, six-five? Six-six? And he's a helluva lot stronger than I am. I'd just guess he intimidates people a little more than I do. Of course he's also a bigger target for people who want to make a name for themselves.

That's why, for me, going out isn't worth the hassle. It's not safe, either. The more you're out there, the more you hang a sign on yourself that says, "Try to take advantage of me." There's always going to be someone who's envious of what you do. Then they get a couple of drinks in them and they want to impress their girlfriend or something. "Watch this, I'm going to go fuck with this guy." So they do. And you know how Charles is. He's not going to take shit from anybody.

People didn't like it when Charles said he wasn't a role model. To a certain extent, we are. But for all the wrong reasons.

A role model is someone you pattern your life after, right? Well, how can you pattern your life after someone you don't know? I don't see how kids can take Michael Jordan or Larry Bird or Barry Bonds or anyone they don't know and try to pattern their lives after him. It's impossible.

Athletes have their quirks and the life we lead is not as glamorous as it seems. And my role models are my parents. They're the ones who raised me. I wouldn't mind being able to hit home runs like Ken Griffey, Jr., or Juan Gonzalez. I'd like to be able to perform in football like Joe Montana or in basketball like Michael Jordan. But that's different from wanting to live my life like them.

At the same time, I know that kids look up to athletes, so I try to watch how I act in public. I try not to get into trouble. But it's up to parents to watch over their kids and set limits, because they're the ones who are with the kids every day. We're not. If I had a son or a daughter who wanted to have a batting stance like Barry Bonds or like Lenny Dykstra, fine. If the kid wanted to have the same pitching motion as Dwight Gooden, fine. But just because you're six years old and you like Lenny Dykstra, you shouldn't start chewing tobacco like Lenny Dykstra. That's where the parent or guardian has to step in.

Some parents, if they knew us, probably wouldn't want us around their kids, much less helping them grow up. Playing sports for a living is like not really growing up. Everyone says baseball is a kid's game, and, honest to God, we're still kids. We're still trying to grow up—or maybe trying not to.

Working double shifts while your wife has to work to help make ends meet—that's being grown up. Making the minimum wage and trying to feed a family of four—that's maturity. That's pressure. We have no pressure. They give us so much money we don't know what to do with it all. That's probably why we're all so screwed up. In a lot of ways we're probably mentally the same age as the kids who are looking up to us.

Anyway, I was talking about hotels. There are only so many hotels you can stay in before you get sick of them. And as I said, the rooms have a desk and a bed. I don't know many people who like to sit at the desk, so you just sort of lie around on the bed because that's all there is to do. Go to the ballpark, go to the hotel. Do that for two or three days and then get on a plane, go to another city and do the same thing. It's a never-ending cycle.

Of course, sometimes we have some fun. One of those times was after we clinched the pennant in Pittsburgh. We didn't get much sleep that night. Darren Daulton is the player representative. He gets a suite on the road, so a bunch of us were down in his room, celebrating. We deserved it. We weren't playing the next day. We weren't driving anywhere. Nobody was going to arrest us for operating an elevator under the influence of alcohol.

There was a bunch of guys staying on the floor below me. And at about seven in the morning, somebody set off the fire alarm. We heard the buzz and the sirens and the voice on the intercom. Most of us had just gotten to sleep—if you call that sleep.

The guys on the floor below me said you could also hear Lenny Dykstra screaming, "Turn that fucking thing off," and so on and so on. If you're in that state and you've just gotten to bed an hour before, it had better be a big damn fire. If it's just a little one, we ain't getting up. It turned out there was a little grease fire in the kitchen or something like that. From our point of view, under those circumstances, if the place wasn't burning down we weren't moving. Unless there were flames coming underneath the door or through the window, I wasn't getting up. I would just take my chances.

It would have been the ugliest team in the world out on the street that morning.

The Phillies don't have a curfew. The Padres did. It was stupid. We had a rule that we had to be in an hour and a half after a game on the road and two hours after a game at home. But they never checked. What were they going to do, go house-to-house? I think it was just something to put on paper so the manager could show the front office that he had discipline.

Sometimes you wake up in the morning and you're in that early morning fog. And you wonder where the hell you are, because all the hotel rooms look the same. Sometimes you have to look at the book to figure out what city you're in.

Sometimes you have no idea what time it is. You look at your watch, but maybe there's been a time change and you have no idea. Sometimes I'll really panic on the road. I'll wake up and I'm not sure what time it is and then I can't remember if we have a day game or a night game.

One time in Philly I got up and went to the stadium. I thought I was real early, but I saw all these cars parked and I thought, "My God, we're playing right now. I'm in trouble." I walked into the clubhouse and there was nobody there. I thought they must all be in the dugout and on the field. I finally found out they were having a high school tournament that day and that was why all the cars were there. I knew I was either really early or really late.

It's better to be really early.

It sounds like a lot of time to kill, but batting practice knocks out about an hour of it. I play cards. Wait for the other guys to come in and start chirping. Talk to the guys who work in the clubhouse. That's what makes it fun going to other cities, seeing those guys again. Maybe I'll get a rubdown, just to have something to do.

From time to time I used to forget what my hotel room number was. Most places we stay, the room number isn't on the key for security reasons. I'd go to the room I thought I was in but the key wouldn't work, and then I'd realize that was the room I was in in the last city. That doesn't happen anymore because I write down the room number on a piece of paper and put it in my wallet so I won't forget.

It's bad enough worrying about having to play without having to try to remember what room you're in, too. I've stopped at the front desk lots of times after getting off a bus or out of a taxi to ask them what room I'm in. What can you do? It sounds funny, but it's an easy thing to have happen.

Heck, I even forget where I live sometimes. I don't have a house in Philadelphia. We stay in a different place each year, and there have been times early in the season when I've gotten lost because I've forgotten exactly where I live.

Getting in some
early practice at
age eighteen months.

Running the bases in
Little League, age eleven.

At Potomac State College,
in 1980. Note the trim
silhouette.

4

With Tony Gwynn in
San Diego, 1987.

Goose Gossage took
John under his wing in
San Diego—and barely
survived a midnight
golf-cart ride in return.

5

Jim Fregosi with Lenny Dykstra,
spring training 1993.

Larry Bowa, whose
reign as manager in San
Diego was stormy to say
the least, was also the
best thing that ever
happened to John.

John smiles with relief
after surviving his All-Star
Game at-bat against
Randy Johnson.

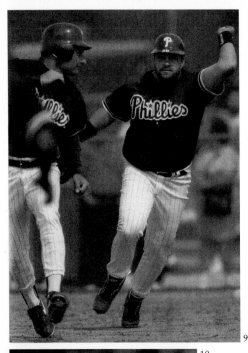

John chases Jim Eisenreich, a.k.a. Jeffrey Dahmer, in a spring rundown drill.

At right:
John bumps chests with Curt Schilling, and is otherwise greeted by *(from left)* Todd Pratt, Tommy Greene, Kim Batiste, and Mitch Williams after his home run in game three of the League Championship Series against Atlanta.

Dave Hollins, who once spared the life of Jim Fregosi—thanks to John's intervention.

John with his father, Moe, and Don Zimmer— Zimmer's the one in uniform.

Curt Schilling hides his face under a towel while Mitch Williams finishes game five against Atlanta.

John's ventilated pants were a fashion highlight of game six of the League Championship Series.

Curt Schilling and Darren Daulton celebrate Schilling's World Series shutout in game five.

Mitch Williams, pitching in
the ninth inning of World
Series game six—his last
inning with the Phillies.

18

John and Jamie,
at the farm.

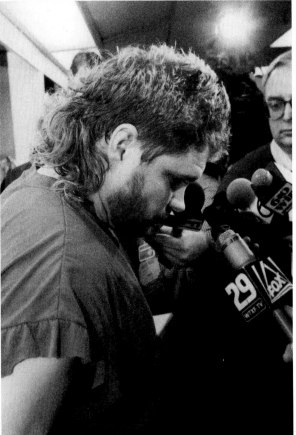

A dejected John
faces the media
after the game
six loss.

I'm not the only one, either. Don Robinson got lost once. He was in Camden and Trenton and everywhere. Sil Campusano lived across the Walt Whitman Bridge from the stadium, and that was the only way he knew how to get there. Well, one day the bridge was closed. He thought if he just went over another bridge he'd be in Philadelphia. But he ended up in Delaware. He saw a sign three times that said Welcome to Delaware. Can you imagine how he felt? He didn't speak English very well, and he was scared to death. When he finally got to the stadium, he was shaking.

But I can see how it happens. When I first got to Philadelphia, I didn't know where the hell I was going. Randy Ready found a place for us, but if Jeff Parrett hadn't been living close by to help me find my way I probably would have done the same thing Sil Campusano did. And if you end up downtown, you're really stuck. I can't drive down there. If I want to go there to eat or something, I just take a cab. Then I'll take another one back to the stadium. I figure the cabdrivers know where they're going.

Of course, it doesn't always work out that way.

One time when I was playing in San Diego, the rest of the team flew to New York. I had to stay behind to get a bunch of X-rays and then fly by myself on the off-day. So there I was, in my first or second year, flying to New York by myself.

I landed just about the time I usually go to the stadium, so I decided to go straight from the airport to the ballpark. I mean, you can see Shea Stadium from La Guardia; it's two minutes away. So I got in a cab and told the driver to take me to Shea Stadium. And he didn't know where it was.

So I asked the cab dispatcher to tell the driver how to get to Shea Stadium. He tried to, but the cabbie didn't speak much English. He really didn't understand. So he took off.

He got lost, of course. We were circling the airport. The meter keeps clicking. I had hardly any money. I hadn't gotten my meal money yet. I wanted to go to the bank, but I'd been in the hospital all day and I didn't have time. I barely caught the plane as it was. And now I'm thinking that I'm going to be on a three-city road trip and I won't even have meal money because this guy is going to run it out.

He kept driving and driving. Finally he got on one road and we could see the stadium. I said, "See that big blue thing? Take me there. That's where I want to go."

Pretty soon we were lost again.

Then I saw the road that I knew would take us to the stadium. I told him to turn, but he wouldn't do it. He kept saying, "I know. I know." And he just kept driving.

I was starting to get pissed.

I started cursing him, yelling and screaming. And all the time the meter kept on clicking. I was thinking I'd have to go in and find someone to borrow money from—if we ever got there.

We finally got there. Somehow. It cost me twenty dollars, and that was after I'd told him to turn the meter off. It was unbelievable. I've gotten in cabs where they've taken me to the wrong stadium. In Chicago, they've tried to take me to Comiskey Park instead of Wrigley Field. In New York one time, the cabbie just started driving. I mentioned that the area didn't look familiar. He said, "You're playing the Yankees, right?" I said, hell no, the Mets.

He said, "Uh-oh."

But the scariest thing I've ever been through on the road was the riots in Los Angeles.

When you play at Dodger Stadium, the place is always packed, even if they're in last place. Even if we're in last place, like we were then. We had just finished taking batting practice when they announced the verdict in the Rodney King trial, that the four policemen who had been accused of beating him had been acquitted. Then they started showing things on TV: the truck driver being beaten, buildings on fire and being looted. Police helicopters were flying over the stadium.

Still, when you're playing a game, you have to think about that. You can't think about what else is going on around you. But when I came up for my last at bat, Mike Scioscia, the Dodgers catcher, stood up. And he said, "Be careful going back to the hotel tonight. Don't even think about going out, because you guys are right in the middle of it and it's getting ugly." He said, "Believe me, you don't want to leave your room."

I grounded back to the pitcher for the last out of the game.

We were getting inning-by-inning accounts. There were guys back in the clubhouse watching on TV. And they'd come to the dugout and say, "Man, you should see what they're doing now. It's a mess out there." There was some devastation.

I think that was the only time I've ever played there where I could hear Vin Scully, the Dodgers broadcaster, announcing my name over the radio, because there was hardly anyone left in the stadium by then.

They were talking about having us just stay in the clubhouse all night and then get up in the morning and flying to San Francisco. You had to figure there was no way we were going to play the next night. The stadium was right where the National Guard was setting up, so we figured it would be safe. Somebody was going to go back to the hotel and pack up all our stuff for us. I was all for that.

I don't know what happened, but they changed their minds. They said, no, we were going back to the hotel because the police had the route blocked off and it should be safe. A bunch of us didn't know what to expect, so we took bats on the bus. I took one just in case. It's not that long a drive, but the streets were quiet. Too quiet. It was unbelievable, like a war zone.

When we got off the bus you could smell the smoke from the burning buildings. I ran into the hotel, ran to my room, and locked the door. I stuck a chair in front of the door.

I stayed up all night watching television. All they had on was stuff about the riots. It was scary. You could hear the sirens. Barry Jones was pitching for us then; some guys were trying to make jokes, and everyone was scared, but Barry Jones, man, he was scared to death. He thought people were going to swing chains and break through the windows of the bus.

The funny thing was, when we got up the next morning to pack, I didn't have anyplace to pack the bat.

Now, they had told us to stay in our rooms and somebody would call the next morning after they'd decided when we were going to leave and how we were going to get to San Francisco. I stayed in my room, but no one called me. Then there was somebody beating on my door, screaming that they were leaving and why wasn't I ready? They said they had tried to call my room, but I was there all day and I never heard the phone ring.

Hell, I was waiting for that phone to ring and tell me something. I hadn't packed, showered, anything, and everybody was down in the lobby waiting for me. Fuck it. I didn't even take a shower. Just threw all my stuff in the suitcase and put on some clothes and just left.

When I got to the lobby, it was crazy. There were rumors that they were canceling flights. There were rumors that the rioters were going to bomb the airport. Darren Daulton said we were going to get a limousine and drive to San Francisco. That was fine with me, but they talked us out of it. We got on a bus and headed for the airport. The trip took forever. And the destruction and burning was right there, right off the freeway where we were driving.

You see it on TV and you think maybe it's just one block or a couple stores. But when you see it in person, it's unbelievable. It was scary, but it was also sad. All that destruction. It's what I've always imagined war must be like. It's something I hope I never see again.

I know it's a cliché, but those riots made baseball seem trivial. Now we were thinking that if we could just get on the plane and get up in the air, we'd be all right. There was a long delay, but the plane finally took off. And everybody was relieved, right? We're going to live. Nobody is going to kill us. We're going to San Francisco and everything will be fine.

Then we got there. They had closed the bridges. People were running around the streets. Oh, man, we were right back in it. We saw a bunch of buildings boarded up. When we get to the hotel in San Francisco there are police out in front to make sure we could get into the lobby safely. There were people outside the barricades yelling, "You're going to die in this city."

Baseball? Didn't seem real important at the moment.

I've always thought of it as a game, but after seeing the riots, I realized that what we do is nothing compared to what some people do with their lives. People died. People got hurt—innocent people. It made me enjoy playing even more because it helped me remember that if I didn't get any hits and we lost, it wasn't the end of the world. Baseball is not a life-or-death situation.

It was like when they had the earthquake during the World Series at Candlestick Park in 1989. I was at home. I had just turned the television on. The earthquake had already happened and one of the first things I saw was Storm Davis standing there holding one of his kids. I had played with him in San Diego, and I'm thinking, "What the hell's going on?"

Then they replayed the start of the show, where Al Michaels says, "Oh, my God, it's an earthquake." That's another situation where it's a tragedy and you understand that people don't really live and die for baseball.

Here are people who have had their homes taken away, and members of their families. What the hell's a baseball game compared to that? Even the World Series. It just ain't that important. I think that's what Mitch Williams was trying to say when people asked him about giving up the home run to Joe Carter. In the end, it's still just a baseball game.

Everyone thinks we're so self-centered, that all we think about is playing baseball and making money. But when you see things like the riot or the earthquake, you're not thinking about any of that. It's too devastating. It's too much of a tragedy.

If somebody came up to me and told me I could never play baseball again, I could live with that. I'll never forget playing baseball, but I could go on. I'm not going to lose a family member over whether I play baseball or not. Baseball isn't the real world. We're in a fantasy land. But tragedies are real. They happen. And they're going to affect people for a long time.

Baseball is a game. Win or lose, you play again the next day. If you lose the last game of the World Series, you can play again next year. It's not the end of the world. For some of those people, the earthquake and the riots really were the end of their world. People are going to remember those things a lot longer than they're going to remember who won the 1993 World Series.

Real life can be painful. Sometimes personal tragedies remind you of that.

There was the car wreck that involved Lenny Dykstra and Darren Daulton. When it happened, it hurt me because it was people I knew. Aside from being teammates, they're also my friends. It didn't help that they got in the accident after leaving a party that had been thrown for me because I was getting married the next day.

We had played a Sunday afternoon game at the Vet, and then a bunch of us went out. Jamie and I got married the next morning at the courthouse, and all the press was there because of the wreck. We were standing there with the judge, and all the reporters were trying to get in. It was a joke. Then I flew to San Diego with the team, and Jamie went back to West Virginia.

All I wanted was to talk to Lenny and Darren. I kept calling the hospital, but they wouldn't put me through. We kept hearing that Lenny might not make it and that Darren might never see again. They have families and baseball is how they support their families. I was so worried that it really didn't matter to me if we won or lost our games against the Padres. None of what was going on around me meant shit to me until I found out they were going to recover and be 100 percent.

It was one of the most upsetting times I've ever had in baseball. It was one of the few times I was so emotionally upset I really didn't care to play. But then I got to thinking that if I didn't play, I would just sit and think about it, and I would get more upset. It was one of those damned-if-you-do and damned-if-you-don't situations. If I didn't play, I knew I'd just feel worse and worse, so I played and tried to block it out of my mind.

It was sad because I couldn't tell anybody what was on my mind. I didn't know if Lenny was going to live or die. I didn't know if Darren would ever be able to see again. I was playing a game where I didn't care if we won or lost; I just wanted to find out how my friends were. But the doctors and nurses wouldn't put me through.

The next day I finally got to talk to them. They both said they were going to be fine. And then I started worrying about what they thought of me. Did they think the accident was my fault because it happened after my party? Deep down, I knew I wasn't to blame. But what did they think? Later, when we got back to Philadelphia, Lenny and Darren came to the clubhouse. They said they didn't blame me for anything, the crash was their own fault. And I was relieved.

Then, last summer, my uncle died. He used to come to a lot of games with my mother and father. He lived near Cleveland. I forget exactly which game it was, but we were behind and then we came back to win. He was watching the game on television and somebody got the hit that won the game for us.

My aunt jumped up and was clapping because we had won the game. Then she looked over, and my uncle just slumped over and died.

I mean, you read in the paper the next day how the Phillies came back and won a game in the bottom of the ninth or whatever, but no one realizes that somebody in your family just died. I didn't even find out until the next day. My brother called me. The Phillies were headed somewhere, and he told me not to come home for the funeral. My aunt, too; she said he would have rather had me playing than missing the game.

It was tough, though. I was upset, but what was I going to do? My aunt said it was best to play, so I went on to Cincinnati. I called her the next day. We talked. It's great to have a comeback win, but games just aren't as important as people think.

I don't want anyone to think I'm complaining about our lifestyle. Playing baseball is a great way to make a living. It's just not as glamorous as people think. They turn on the television one night and we're playing in, say, Houston. Then they tune in the next night and we're in Montreal. But they don't stop to think what went on in between. Checking out of one hotel and into another. The plane flight. The bus rides. It's not exactly glamorous.

And as for those museums and historical sights that I haven't gotten around to seeing on the road? Maybe I'll see them when I'm through playing. But probably not.

**The question people ask most
often is "What's David Letterman
really like?"**

12

SOMETIMES WHEN I READ THE NEWSPAPER

I pick up the entertainment section. I read about this guy or
this group, and I think it would be fun to meet some of them.

I guess entertainers do the same thing. The Phillies got a lot
of publicity last year, some of it not so good, but we were
getting noticed, and a lot of people were impressed by that.

They picked up a sports section or a magazine, saw a story about the Phillies, and said, "Man, I'd like to meet these guys." And some of them did.

The first time I really thought about that was when I was with the Padres. Goose Gossage and Willie Nelson were friends. They were so tight that Willie Nelson scheduled a concert in Yuma, Arizona, while we were in spring training. He told his manager to get him a concert in Yuma so he could see Goose.

We had a lot more people like that come into the clubhouse last year, when we were winning, than we had before. But I'll always have a soft spot for the guys who didn't wait until we were hot. Sawyer Brown, they were with us even when we were in last place. They were friends of Mitch Williams. They've been around us a lot. The lead singer, Mark Miller, even flew up to Atlanta from Florida during the playoffs just to bring me an autographed picture of Dolly Parton.

It's my prized possession.

I haven't gotten it framed yet. My wife won't let me put it up. Dolly Parton has always been my favorite. Not just because she's, um, well endowed but because I like her music. I told that to the guys in Sawyer Brown one time, and they said, "Would you like her autograph?" I couldn't believe they knew her.

But I guess that's the same as somebody saying they couldn't believe that I knew Lenny Dykstra or Barry Bonds or whoever. Here are guys who play in the band with Steely Dan or Billy Joel or Sawyer Brown, and they come in and it's like, "Oh, man, I can't believe I'm here. I really wanted to meet you guys." It's kind of awkward at first, because they don't know what to say to us—and we sure as hell don't know what to say to them. But after a while you realize that we're all just people who happen to entertain other people for a living. We're normal.

Well, sort of normal. As far as normal in that world goes.

I could never have imagined being on David Letterman's show. I really don't know how it happened the first time, back in 1992. All I know is that Larry Shenk, our vice president for public relations, came down to the clubhouse one day and said they'd gotten a call from the Letterman show, and they wanted me to be on.

I figured, what the hell? I mean, we were in last place. You gotta have one highlight in a season. So I figured I'd go and talk to him. And it was fun.

I was reluctant at first. I didn't think I really wanted to. It wasn't the kind of thing I'd normally do. But my wife had a little bit to say about it. Lenny Dykstra had been on it and he told me to go ahead, that I would enjoy myself. And I did.

I had watched the show fairly regularly. I knew that a few years earlier Letterman had called Terry Forster, the pitcher, a fat tub of goo. I was a little worried about that. I didn't know if he was going to bury me or make fun of me or what, but it was all done in good taste.

They sent a limo down to Philly and drove me to New York. I was nervous all the way up. But once the show started, I really didn't want it to end. You drive all the way up there, two hours. Then you're on for five minutes. And all the way back I was thinking that wasn't long enough. You know, if you're going to drive for two hours, you ought to be on for at least an hour.

Letterman seemed like a normal person. He was really funny during the break. He leaned over and said, "You know, this band really sucks. What the hell kind of music was that?" He was talking about the group they had booked. It cracked me up. I started laughing because I was thinking the same thing, but I wasn't going to say anything. He says, "My own fucking show and I can't get any better music than this." It was hilarious.

After the show he came back and talked to us for a while. They said he'd never done that before, that he usually left as soon as the show was over, but he came back and talked and that was nice.

Letterman's people called again last year and I went on again, pretty soon after he started on CBS. I didn't want to do it the second time, I really didn't. But they kept calling, and people from the front office kept asking me to do it, saying it would be good, that sort of thing.

Finally the producers caught me one day when I would have agreed to just about anything. I said I'd do it. But the day before, I asked them to call and see if I could cancel. By then we were in a pennant race. It was my first day off in a while, we were at home, and I just wanted to relax. I didn't want to spend the whole off-day driving to and from New York.

They tried to get Dave Winfield, because he had just gotten his three thousandth hit, but he had something else to do. They said I was stuck. So I had to go.

The interview turned out fine. But I was nervous on the way up again. I was thinking, What am I going to say? What if I screw up? I don't like that feeling. I can play baseball in front of fifty thousand people in the stands and millions on television and that's fine, but I'm nervous sitting there talking to one guy. Letterman's the only person you can see. The theater's dark, and only the stage is lit up, so you can't see the audience at all. You just sit there and talk. And it's nerve-racking.

I had some idea of what was coming though. The producer had called me every day for a week. "Can you think of something to talk about?" So I'd tell him a couple things that had happened, and he'd say, "We'll use that." But you don't know exactly what's going to happen when the show starts. The thing is to keep Letterman off guard. Make him think harder than you're thinking.

Then when you're driving up there you forget what the hell

you told the producer you were going to say. But it probably comes off better that way, when you have to think of something real quick.

We were supposed to do a skit. We didn't do it for some reason, but the way it was supposed to work is that Belinda Carlisle was going to throw baseballs off the roof of the Ed Sullivan Theater and David Letterman and I were supposed to catch them. I was just standing there by myself and people were driving by, honking their horns, waving.

The one thing I did the second time was dress comfortably. The first time I had dressed up. Lenny told me I had to wear a suit; I didn't want to, so I wore slacks and a shirt and dress shoes. I thought that was the way it was supposed to be. The next time I told them that I didn't want to dress up and they said they didn't care, that I could wear whatever I wanted.

It just so happened that Steely Dan came in to see us the night before. They knew I was going to be on Letterman, and I said that if they had a T-shirt I'd wear it on the show. Give them some airtime. So one guy gave me the shirt off his back. Well, if a man gives you the shirt off his back, you have to wear it, right? So I took it home and my wife washed it. Then I got to thinking that you can't wear dress pants with a T-shirt. So I decided to wear jeans. Then I realized that if I was going to do this for Steely Dan, I had to give Sawyer Brown some airtime, too, so I wore one of their hats.

I'm sure there were people in our front office who weren't too pleased with the way I dressed. They probably thought I looked like a slob. But I made the man a promise and I kept my promise. And besides, I was comfortable, and it gave Letterman something to start with; when I came out, he said, "First of all, thanks for fixing yourself up tonight."

I knew they were going to do something about me chewing a lot of gum, because they had film clips of me with a whole lot of gum stuffed in my mouth. That's one of my superstitions, and all I can say about it is that at least it's better than when I was chewing tobacco. I told Letterman that when the dentist keeps pulling your teeth, you have to give up something, and I figured the sugar was going to cause less damage than the tobacco. I think I might have blown a bubble gum endorsement right there.

Then he asked me about playing games in Denver, if I liked it there. That was something I'd talked about with the producers; I told him I didn't like it for one reason: there's no air. And I told him about a recent game there: "I was on base and there was a three-and-two count. Two outs. So they made me run. And Dave Hollins kept fouling balls off. And I kept getting more tired.

"I told the first base coach, I said, 'I'm not going.'

"He said, 'Well, you have to.'

"I said, 'The hell I do.' "

Letterman asked me, "That's the way the game is played, I think. Isn't it?"

"Yeah," I said, "but I was going to bend the rules there for a while. So then he hit a ball in the gap and I had to try to score. And I slid into home, but it really wasn't much of a slide because I had no momentum left. It was just kind of a *stick*. And I was safe, and Darren Daulton had to pick me up and help me back to the dugout."

That got some pretty good laughs.

Then he asked me about my number, 29, and why I had it, and I told him about my deal with Mitch Williams: "I had number twenty-eight, and we made a trade for Mitch Williams. And I saw where Rickey Henderson gave a guy twenty-five thousand dollars for his number. Well, I got two cases of beer. . . . [Mitch] wanted twenty-eight [because] his wife had a bunch of jewelry with number twenty-eight on it. . . . The best part about it is, now he got divorced. Now he wears number ninety-nine. And the two cases of beer are gone."

Letterman said, "Oh, that's too bad."

And I shook my head and said, "It's a sad story."

Everybody seemed to like that line, and the audience laughed and clapped. Then finally I told him about playing cards with Larry Bowa, and how I suck at spades and owe him about $10,000 for the season—but it's not really gambling, because I'm not paying him. And that was about it. I thought it went pretty well.

This winter that whole bit was nominated for some award from ESPN for outstanding performance by an athlete in an entertainment role or something. That's when you know there are too many awards and things, when they start giving them out for how you did on a talk show. The other nominees were a Shaquille O'Neal rap song about dunking on people, and a skit with Charles Barkley playing one-on-one with Barney. Now, I can see coming in second to Shaq, and I like Charles, but really, I better not lose to that purple thing. I'd have to take some serious heat about that.

I watch Letterman's show more than ever now because I've spoken to him. It's more special. And I know it's a big deal, because the question people ask me most often is "What's David Letterman really like?"

He's a guy who would fit right into our clubhouse, I'll tell you that. He'd jump right into the fray, right into the insanity. He would fit in so good it wouldn't be like guys on the team would say, "Oh, man, that's David Letterman." It would be more like, "Oh, there's Dave."

He's the kind of guy you could rag if he had a bad show or if he said something stupid, and he'd come right back at you. And he knows what's going on in sports. He has a pretty good idea about baseball. He's probably an ex-jock who didn't make it and said, "I can be just as fucked up as them. I'm going to get a show." I'd love for him to come into our clubhouse someday and just sit down and b.s. with us. He could hang with us.

So there are some advantages to being a ballplayer. You

meet some people you probably wouldn't get to meet otherwise, and you can sit and b.s. and tell stories.

Tom Selleck came one time and took batting practice with us. He put on a uniform and then he sat in the clubhouse and we talked for a while. That was fun. You read so much stuff about Hollywood and entertainers and how stuck-up they are and all that, how they think they're better than everyone else. And then you meet them and they're just, you know, people. They have a talent and they use it.

I don't understand how people can get jealous of how much money they make—or how much money we make. People see us playing games, but they don't realize how much we travel and how much time we spend away from home. They don't think about the years in the minors and the hard work it took to get to this point of our careers. It's the same with actors; people see a two-hour movie, but the actors might have been on location in a foreign country for a year, living in a hut. People just see the finished product, and they don't realize what it took to get there.

I have to admit, though, that I was shocked to see that Barbra Streisand was getting $10 million to do a concert in Las Vegas. I mean, damn. She's talented, but, wow.

It's funny. A lot of the bands that came to the clubhouse this year, it seemed like they were more in awe of meeting us than we were of meeting them. We realized after a while that they were just regular folks. And I imagine that maybe, after they left, some of those guys told people, "I met John Kruk, and you know what? He's just like us."

Sometimes my wife and I go out to dinner and people just stare. It makes me feel like one of those rare lions in the zoo. I hope they're not waiting for me to crap all over the place like the lions do.

I mean, it's hard to eat with people watching you. You don't want to drip food down your chin or onto your shirt. They just keep looking at you, and there's nothing you can do about it.

It's nice being noticed—a certain amount. It opens the door to other things. But sometimes I wish people would think about why they go to a restaurant or a bar or a movie. They go to eat or have a drink or see the movie. That's the same reason we go there. Not to sign autographs.

I understand why people like autographs. I was thrilled when I got that picture signed by Dolly Parton. But it's getting real out of control.

I never asked for autographs when I was a kid. I was too shy. I didn't know how to go about it. I think the first one I ever got was from Andre Dawson, when I was a player—and I still felt bad about asking for it. I got one from Nolan Ryan, but I had somebody else get it for me; a guy I had played with in the minors, Billy Hatcher, asked him. He didn't mind. I was like, "Shit, I can't ask him. That's *Nolan Ryan*. Some dumb kid his first year in the big leagues don't go up to Nolan Ryan and ask for his autograph." I'd like to have Mike Schmidt's. He's around every once in a while. But he doesn't come in to sign autographs for us idiots.

It's a lot different now that we've been in the playoffs and World Series. You feel like a freak when you go out in public. You go out and people stare and whisper. "That's so-and-so." It makes you feel real uncomfortable because you don't know if they like you, if they respect the way you play, or if they want to kill you. You get real leery.

I try to sign as much as I can. The only time it's really bad is when you're trying to eat. You just got done cutting a piece of steak or whatever and you're getting ready to put it into your mouth and someone just comes along and throws a paper at you. So you think, "Well, I'll just sign this one."

But then it's like you've got a bull's-eye on your ass and everyone can take a shot. Open season, come and get it. That's when it's real inconvenient. Or maybe you're out somewhere, just trying to have a conversation, and you feel like you have to include everybody who comes over in the conversation, because people keep coming over and if you stopped talking every time, you'd be there all night. So you feel like you have to watch what you say. There's no privacy anymore.

The only time you have any privacy is in your room. That's why I'm the king of room service. And even then, if you don't put a block on your phone, you'll get calls at all hours, five o'clock or six o'clock in the morning, from radio stations all over wanting you to do their sports talk show.

They all say they just want five minutes. I tell them I was asleep and that they woke me up. They say it will only take five minutes, that it won't be bad. Maybe not for them, but I asked one guy, I said, "Would you like me to call you at five o'clock in the morning if you just got back at two o'clock because you played a night game? Would you want me to call you after you'd been asleep for three hours and want to interview you for five minutes?"

They don't understand. They think they're the only ones who ever call. But they're not. Last year it happened just about every day until I started putting a block on the line.

One time after that, the phone rang real early in the morning. I thought, "Oh, shit, someone died," because I'd told the desk not to put any calls through unless it was an emergency or somebody from my family. So the phone rang and the operator said it was my uncle. I told them to put the call through.

And then some guy comes on the line: "Sorry to bother you, but will you go on our show?" I said a few choice six-in-the-morning curse words and hung up the phone. Jeez. What can you do? It's not the hotel's fault.

Some people didn't think it was right for Cal Ripken, Jr., to stay at a different hotel, under an assumed name, apart from the rest of the Orioles. But I can understand why he did that.

He's one of those larger-than-life players. He does milk commercials. The whole thing. He's like Dale Murphy. Everyone likes him. I read an article that said some of his teammates didn't think it was right. Who cares? As long as he shows up and plays and plays hard, there shouldn't be any complaining. I mean, if he wanted to commute from Baltimore and fly back and forth every night, what's wrong with that?

I think he's on to something that's coming, though; if things keep going the way they are, in twenty years you'll probably see twenty-five different players staying in twenty-five different hotels, all under assumed names. There won't be a team hotel anymore. That's a bad thing. But the team hotels are listed and the card collectors know them.

I've had people drop off big envelopes at the hotel. The desk clerk puts the message light on and says I have a package. I think it might be from my agent or someone, so I go down and it's an envelope full of pictures with a pen and a little note that says, "Sign these and leave them in the lobby." And the fan's name is on another envelope. You know, that's being pretty forward. A lot of times I just put the pictures in the other envelope with his name on it; I leave it, but I don't sign the pictures, because if I do it once, who's to say there won't be more pictures from him the next day?

In Philly, if somebody finds out where you live, stuff gets left in the mailbox. Sign this, sign that.

I don't mind signing an autograph for a kid, but I've seen adults push kids out of the way to get autographs. That's when I stop. That's rude. You don't push kids out of the way. A kid will come up to me with a crumpled card I know he can't sell; he wants the autograph for himself. Some adults come up to me with a stack of cards and special pens, and they push the kids out of the way; it's obvious they want to sell them. That's when I take a hike.

I know a lot of people think ballplayers are all inconsiderate assholes, but we've reached the point with all this stuff that it's hard not to be rude, because it goes on around us every single day. Television magnifies everything, makes us seem larger than life, so fans forget we're still people. I've never felt larger than life. Wider, maybe, but not larger.

That's another reason Dale Murphy was so amazing. He was always nice. I don't know how he lasted so long in this game. I think you've got to be an asshole to a certain point—because, if you're not, people will run right over you.

The guys in the front office are always asking us to do stuff. A lot of us might just say, "Fuck it, I ain't doing it." With Murf, it was always "Sure. Let's go. Let's do it now." Of course, he didn't play cards; a lot of the stuff they want us to do cuts into our card-playing time, so we just can't do it.

When I think of great baseball players, I think of guys like Nolan Ryan and Andre Dawson, guys who played a lot of years and put up great numbers. Pete Rose, Mike Schmidt, Steve Carlton—I'm in awe of those people. I still feel like I play in a semipro league and those are the guys who play on TV.

Maybe I'll sit back one day and realize I'm in the big leagues too. Maybe I'll look at the pictures I have from All-Star games: me and Barry Bonds, me and Fred McGriff, me and Ken Griffey, Jr. Maybe someday I'll say, "Man, I played with those guys, against those guys." But not now. I mean, I was scared to death to talk to Dale Murphy at first. I was scared to death to talk to Ryne Sandberg. Sometimes I still feel like I shouldn't be on the same field with guys like that.

It's so hard for me to understand why some people seem to be jealous of us. Like I said, the recognition is nice, but sometimes people get a little weird.

One time I got a letter from a guy who wanted me to send him $10,000. Just like that. Said he needed it.

Last season a reporter went to my hometown. He talked to a lot of people who told him things about me. I read the article, and one of the people he talked to, I have no idea who he is. I don't think I've ever seen him in my life.

I guess the reporter just went into a bar and asked if anybody knew me. You know how it is when someone has a couple drinks: "Yeah, I know him." He wants to get his name in the paper. The next thing you know, this guy is telling the reporter about how he's always up at my house, parties with me all the time. And then he starts talking about how I drive around in a big white Mercedes, I'm so cocky, all this stuff. Well, I don't have a big white Mercedes. Maybe I seem cocky, but I think that's because I'm being careful. People think we should stop to talk to everyone, but really, we don't know what they're going to do.

There are so many rumors about me back home. That I bought everything in town. I bought the golf course. There's a new bowling alley; it's mine. A friend of mine owns a bar; that's mine, too. I'm just letting him run it. But I don't. I own a farm, two houses, and two cars. That's all.

Jamie and I are also getting a divorce. Because I'm gay. And she's on drugs and having an affair.

One of the best ones was when my wife and I and some of our friends went out to a little bar we go to. We sat there for four or five hours, then went home.

The next morning I was in town and I saw my mom and dad. My mom says, "Where's Darren Daulton?"

I said, "What?"

She said, "Where's Darren?"

I said, "What are you talking about?"

She goes, "Oh, my God. Some woman called me at eight o'clock this morning just to tell me that she saw you and Darren out with two strange women last night."

You know, everyone has seen me everywhere. I've done everything there is to do. And really, I don't do anything. There are a few friends I do things with a lot, and if I'm not out with them, or if me and Jamie don't go out by ourselves, then I don't go—because those are the only people I feel comfortable around.

I know a lot of people back home talk behind my back,

which is fine. I don't care. But don't start spreading shit. If you want to think I'm stuck-up or I'm an asshole or whatever, that's fine, but don't start saying that my wife's on drugs, she's having an affair, we're getting divorced because I'm gay. That's just childish.

The people who spread rumors like that, they aren't my friends. They probably never were my friends. But there are plenty of people who, when I go home, accept me for being myself. We play golf, we play basketball, go hunting, whatever. Those are the people who've treated me the same from back when I was in high school and the minor leagues until now. That's all I ask.

I guess it's part of the price you pay for living in a small town. You know just about everyone. And some of them—not all, but some—think, I work eight hours a day and he makes all that money. I work and he comes home in the winter and he doesn't have to work, just does what he wants, can buy whatever he wants." It's jealousy. "Why did he get that and I didn't?" Every day I meet someone who says his kid wants to grow up and be a baseball player and be on television like me. The first thing I think is, Well, I hope that happens, because that will take a lot of the pressure off me.

You know, I'd be happy if everyone in our town made more money than me. I really would. It wouldn't matter to me. I don't go back there to show off; I go back there because that's where I live.

Sometimes, though, things can get a little scary.

One day this winter I was out at my farm with a couple friends. We were messing around, cutting some wood. And somebody fired a gun over our heads—not once but five or six times.

Now, it could have been one of two things. They were on my land. They might have been hunting and didn't know it was my land, even though it's posted with No Trespassing signs. Or maybe they just wandered in and they were hunting and they heard the chain saws. So maybe they thought we were scaring the deer, so they shot above us to make us stop.

But, you know, one or two shots, okay. But five or six is not an accident.

So then I started thinking maybe it was somebody who didn't like me, because the two guys I was with are the nicest guys in the world. They've never done nothing wrong to no one.

Maybe I'm paranoid, but I don't think so. You look at what happened to Monica Seles. You look at what happened to Nancy Kerrigan. There are idiots who run onto the field at baseball games all the time. How can you be sure they're not going to try to hurt somebody? You see something happen to another athlete, see somebody get hurt by a fan, and you have to think about how it could have been you.

There had to be a reason for those shots. That's our property. That's our farm. I'm not going to let some guy who doesn't like me run me off, so when I go out there now, I go prepared. All I had was a chain saw. What do you want me to do, chase a guy down with a chain saw? No. I take a gun.

I still don't know what happened. It could have been just somebody messing around. But a gun is nothing to mess around with.

The one guy I was with, I'd never seen him get excited about anything, never. And he was actually scared. It scared me to see him like that, because he's the kind of guy, if he cut off his finger, he'd just say, "Well, it looks like I'll have to go to the hospital."

If somebody doesn't like me and wants to shoot at me, I'm up at the farm alone a lot. Why don't they do it then? Why bring other people into it? Because if any of my friends ever get hurt because of me, well, I probably shouldn't say it, but if somebody shoots at me again, or at anyone in my family or any of my friends, if I ever find him I'll kill him. If that's bad, that's bad.

If someone shoots at me, I'll shoot back. If that's wrong, that's wrong. But what am I supposed to do? Run to the truck, jump in, and go find the police? They're not going to find him by then.

I really hate having to think about things like that. In a lot of ways life was simpler back when I was making $700 a month playing in Reno. I get a kick out of what my life is like, and I do like being noticed. Really. And I'm not complaining about my life. But sometimes people go too far. I mean, Mitch Williams got death threats. Monica Seles got stabbed. How long is it going to be before some crazy fan hurts a baseball player? People send us cookies all the time. Would you eat them? It's getting to the point where it's hard to trust anybody, and the fans are the ones who'll lose out, because the players are going to be more and more reluctant to stop in a crowd.

The umpire said, "You're a little young to be pulling that foot off, aren't you?"
I said, "Yes, sir."

DURING THE WORLD SERIES, CBS USED AN overhead camera above home plate. The umpires went ballistic because it showed that they missed a call every now and then. They bitched and moaned.

Well, umpires do a good job. Most of them do. But they also have egos. They don't want to be overruled. They really didn't want people all over the world seeing them missing calls. Players complain about calls, and sometimes we have the right to do it. Most of the time we probably don't have a right to say anything, but sometimes we complain and we're right. Doesn't do any good, of course.

I think the umpires tried to get rid of that camera because they don't want to admit that they miss a few. They don't want it proven.

One thing nobody really brought up, though, was that most hitters don't mind when an umpire calls a strike on a pitch that's six inches outside. As long as that same pitch is a strike all night long, as long as he's consistent, we just figure, if the guy has a wide plate, he has a wide plate. We can deal with that. But if the same pitch is a strike one time and a ball another time, that's when it really gets bad.

As players we're expected to be consistent, and we expect the same thing from the umpires. If there's going to be a big strike zone, do it all the time. If the pitch on the outside corner is a ball, call it a ball all day. We really appreciate that.

Most of the umpires don't talk a lot. They're usually pretty guarded. But I've seen a few funny things happen with the men in blue.

We played a game against the Mets at Veterans Stadium last year. Mitch Williams was pitching in the ninth inning, and he didn't like some of the calls. Jim Fregosi came and took him out of the game. As long as Mitch was getting taken out anyway, he figured he might as well get thrown out.

As he was walking back to the dugout he got into an argument with Jim Quick, the home plate umpire. Mitch said something and Quick said something. Then Mitch said, "Kiss my ass."

And Quick said, "Pick a spot. You're all ass."

I thought that was a pretty funny line.

The Phillies have had some trouble with umpires over the

years. We've had problems with Joe West. Von Hayes, especially, had problems, but you can understand why. Hayes complained about everything—every call, every pitch. He really complained.

Lenny Dykstra had a run-in with West, too. He wanted West to move to the other side of second base so he could pick up the ball better. You would think it would be common courtesy, but West didn't want to move.

The bad thing is, there's nothing you can do. Umpires have got a strong union and they don't work on a merit system. They can be as bad as they want for as long as they want and it seems like some of them just don't care. They know they'll be back.

If a player is bad enough for long enough, he's gone. If the umpires had the same fear, maybe they'd bear down a little more. I'm not saying all of them, just a few. Most of them do what they have to. They hustle and they get into the right position. With a few of them, though, it's like they think the fans come out to watch them, and I don't think that's the right way to be.

For most of his career, Doug Harvey was a good umpire. He was called God. They were calling him that long before I got there. But he was human.

He was always good when we'd get him behind the dish in spring training in Arizona, where it's real hot and dry. Every time you came to bat, the first time up for every hitter, he'd lean over and say, "It's a good day to swing the bat, son." And you had to. And that's all right, there.

Harvey was funny. He talked to me all the time. Maybe he'd called me out on a pitch I thought was outside. The next at bat I'd walk up to him. I'd want to be polite, him being God and all, but I'd ask him, "Do you think that pitch might have been a little outside?" And he'd say, "I'm going to teach you how to hit that pitch."

So I'm standing there thinking, Ted Williams couldn't teach me how to hit a pitch that far outside. I thought it was just a bad call. But what are you going to do?

Some people think that making the strike zone bigger would be a good way to speed up games. It might. It might prolong them, too, because everyone would be arguing. The strike zone is so inconsistent as it is right now. Each umpire has his own strike zone. So if a guy is notorious for not calling the outside pitch a strike, how are you going to tell him to all of a sudden widen out his zone?

These guys have patterns just like we do. We know that when a certain umpire is behind the plate, he doesn't call the outside pitch, so we lay off of it. If one day you have to start swinging at it, it will take time to adjust. And I think it would be even harder for the umpires.

They've tried to mess with the strike zone, but ever since I've been in the league, it's been pretty much the same: belt buckle to the top of the knees. That's fine with me—the smaller the better. Umpires are programmed to call it that way. You can't really ask them to change. That would be like asking me or Lenny Dykstra or Darren Daulton to bat right-handed. We couldn't do it.

How you approach an at bat depends to some extent on who the umpire is. Frank Pulli has a reputation for having a big strike zone, maybe the biggest in the league. Large. Maybe extra large. When he's back there, I know I have to go up there swinging, but he's always been like that and that's the way it is. That's life.

Tom Hallion is real consistent. Dana DeMuth has a real consistent strike zone from game to game. Charlie Williams is such a nice guy that you really can't argue with him. Still, he was the first umpire who ever threw me out of a game, in Chicago.

It was a called third strike and I argued. Now, there's a right way and a wrong way to argue. For a rookie, there's no right way. For older guys, the best way is just to ask, quietly so no one else can tell, "Do you think that pitch might have been a little outside?" Some umpires will even admit it. They'll say they might have missed it. Then it's over and done, and you go about your business. But if you turn around, even if you ask nicely, they'll probably say something like "That's a good fucking pitch. Get in there and swing the bat."

You always hear that if you're young and get thrown out of a game the umpire will hold a grudge against you, but Charlie's been real nice to me. I don't have a real good read on his strike zone just yet, but it's only been eight years. Maybe in a couple more years I'll zero in on it.

I really believe that umpires test young players. I thought Kevin Stocker got some bad calls this year, but he handled it the right way. He just turned and walked away. He never threw his helmet or his bat. That took a lot of restraint.

I thought he was too calm, but guys who had played with him in the minors told me, no, wait until he gets settled in a little bit. Then he'll start snapping. I hope I'm around to see that. I think the umpires tested him last year by ringing him up on some pitches that weren't strikes. Well, maybe they weren't strikes to someone else, but they were strikes to Stocker. I guess the umpires wanted to see if he could handle it. And he handled it well. I think he got their respect.

Managers test young players. So I guess there's no reason why umpires wouldn't, too.

My first spring training, I had a run-in with Paul Runge. I had finished playing in an exhibition game against the Cubs, and I was doing my running in the outfield. I got to the right field foul line, where the Cubs bullpen was, and Lee Smith started talking to me. I started to say something. And Paul Runge, who was at first base, came down the line and told me to get the hell out of there.

I said, "What the hell's wrong with you?" But he just kept telling me to get the hell out of there. So I took off, and when I finished my running I asked Tim Flannery what Runge's problem was. And he said, "He's testing you. And don't cross him, or he'll stick it up your ass." I said, "Okay, I've got it." And Paul Runge and I have had a pretty good relationship since then.

One time I turned around and asked about a pitch. The umpire snapped at me. I called him a dick. He didn't throw me out, though. He should have. But I think he realized he had done something wrong first. I guess two wrongs made a right in that case because he let me stay in the game.

Some umpires are really belligerent. They can say things that really piss you off, but if you say the same thing back to them, you're gone. That's not right, but there's nothing we can do. We don't get to file reports like they do.

When I say belligerent, I mean if he makes a bad call, or even a borderline call, and you just ask, nicely, something like, "Do you think that pitch was a little outside?" or "Is it possible you missed that call, because I really thought he was out?" And they say, "Fuck you" or "Shut your mouth and throw the ball back to the pitcher and let's get going."

Granted, we don't always ask that politely. But I've asked nicely sometimes and had them answer me belligerently. It makes you wonder why. You only asked the man a question. If he just says he thought it was a strike or he thought the runner beat the throw, fine; you accept it and you go on. But when he answers like that, the first thing in your mind is that he's trying to screw you.

The umpires might say it's a judgment call, but there's a judgment from both sides. If you're in court you have a right to argue your side in a civil way, but not in baseball. Sometimes they just give you that little laugh and that smirk—not most of them, just a few; I want to stress that—and that just doesn't seem right.

I can see things from the umpire's point of view, though. If we're considered good hitters, we still fail seven out of ten times. The umpires have to be a lot better than that. If a pitch is coming in at 90 miles an hour, we only have a split second to decide whether to swing or take. They have that same amount of time to call it a ball or a strike.

I think all the cameras and instant replays put more pressure on them, too. If there's a bang-bang play and they miss it, it's going to be all over TV from six different angles.

If you're going to argue, whether you get thrown out or not depends a lot on how you do it. Say you think a guy made a bad call at first. If you say, "That's horseshit" or "That's a horseshit call," they usually won't throw you out. But if you say, "*You're* horseshit," you're gone. You can curse, unless you get real vulgar, but if you make it a personal thing, book it. You'll be in the clubhouse before long.

There are a few umpires you just don't argue with. You let it slide. If there's a close play at first and the next inning you're standing almost right next to the first base umpire, sometimes you can just ask. You know, just talk about it. You get a better understanding. But if the umpire just walks away and doesn't even want to talk about it, you think maybe he knows he was wrong.

Sometimes it doesn't matter what you do or say, though. We were playing in Atlanta once. It was real hot and miserable. Eric Gregg called Lenny Dykstra out at second on a stolen base attempt. Well, Lenny argued. And argued and argued and argued. Then, after the inning, he was running out to center field and he argued some more. But he didn't get thrown out.

After he got out to his position, Eric looked into our dugout. "He's not coming out of this game," he said. "If I've got to stay out in this heat, he does, too."

There are some managers, I think, who go out to argue with the idea of getting thrown out, or at least firing their team up, the way basketball coaches sometimes get technical fouls.

When I was in San Diego, we never knew whether Larry Bowa was doing that or not. Larry's such a psycho that he probably wasn't. A bunch of us got a big kick out of watching him, though. We'd sit there in the dugout and hit the guy next to us and say, "Look at him. He's going to have a heart attack." Bowa really got excited. I think some managers would argue because their team might be dead or going through a losing streak or something. They might think they need something to get them going. So they go out and argue about something silly.

But I don't think that works. The manager isn't pitching, hitting, or fielding for you. In basketball, getting a technical might help because it slows down the other team's momentum. What kind of momentum is there in baseball? Pretty much slow, slower, and slowest. That's it.

As much as I can appreciate what a tough job umpires have, I have to admit that at times I try to make their job just a little tougher.

Like coming off first base a little quicker on a close play. Or giving a long stretch with my foot a couple inches off the bag. Steve Garvey taught me that one. Of course, the first time I tried it the umpire said, "You're a little young to be pulling that foot off, aren't you?"

I said, "Yes, sir." Steve Garvey did it all the time, but he was Steve Garvey. He'd been around forever.

There are other things players do to make it more difficult for umpires. Tony Gwynn may hate me for saying this, but if you ever watch him hit, he stands up so far in the batter's box that when he strides his front foot is over the front line. But he hits .330 or .340 every year, so everybody just kind of lets it slide. I've never heard anybody say anything about it.

Other guys like to stay as far back as is legal, or even a little farther. It's easier to erase the back line than the front line. I know there have been times when I feel my bat's real slow and the pitcher is throwing real hard, so I've tried to knock out a little bit of that line and step back a couple inches. It probably doesn't help, but mentally you think the ball won't get there quite as quick.

Then there are catchers who frame the ball. They set up six inches outside and the pitcher hits the glove and it's called a strike. Ted Simmons used to do that to me all the time when we were playing the Braves. He'd set up outside—strike one. A little farther outside—strike two. I just looked at him one time and said, "I guess when I get a little older I won't get those, huh?"

Catchers can do a lot. On breaking balls, instead of reaching out and catching them, they can let them come back in and catch them more with their body. Bruce Benedict used to be real good at that. The ball crosses the plate above your chest but by the time he catches it, it's down around your knees. He got a lot of calls that way. So did Bob Boone.

Another reason I feel sorry for umpires is that they're always on the road. We're gone half the month, but at least we're home half the month. All they get is a two-week vacation in the middle of the summer. If they don't live in a city where there's a team, they're gone almost the whole summer.

And there's another point. Every half inning we get to go into the dugout to cool off or warm up. We can run up to the clubhouse. They have to stand out there the whole time. It's not an easy job.

Overall, umpires do a great job. I'd say that 99 percent of the time they give it everything they've got. But I would like to see some kind of evaluation system put in.

There was a lot of talk about that at the All-Star game and at the World Series. If an umpire makes the same mistake over and over, you just wish there was some way it could be corrected. If a player is being moved from the infield to the outfield or a pitcher is working on a new pitch, he goes to the Instructional League. Maybe they could have something like that for umpires. You know it's impossible, but you just wish there was some way to get it done, because the way it is, they're too secure; they know they can't get fired.

And I wish they wouldn't be so touchy about having their calls questioned and about overhead cameras and all that stuff. Players aren't expected to be perfect. Umpires can't be expected to be perfect either.

I've worn some hideous uniforms in my life.

SAY LENNY DYKSTRA GETS A DOZEN NEW
bats. He might pick out one or two that he likes and the rest of them he gets rid of. You might wonder why, but he's just got that feeling.

I've seen times when the trademark on the bat wasn't lined up just right with his name, so he got rid of the whole order.

He said he didn't like the fact that when he was in the batter's box and he looked down at his bat, it wasn't lined up. That might seem strange. But if you'll remember, he had a hell of a time early in the 1993 season. He really struggled until they finally sent him some bats he liked. And then he got hot and hit for the rest of the year. I didn't used to think something like that could matter, but maybe it does. Any little thing that's different from normal can throw you out of sync. And that threw him out of sync bad.

Of course, I'm not one to talk. There are times I can't remember my whole phone number but I can tell you exactly which pair of socks I wore with my uniform the night before and just how I wore them. That's a little scary. I'm thinking about stuff like that when there are probably a lot more important things to worry about. So I guess my priorities are pretty screwed up, too.

It's just that, when you play every day, there are so many ups and downs. Football, they play once a week. It's probably hard for them to remember from one game to the next what they did, so they maybe don't have as many superstitions. Basketball and hockey, they play a couple times a week, but they have days off in between. But in baseball, we play almost every day. And I think that's why we have so many superstitions.

I wear a different batting glove in batting practice than I do in the game, though I try to wear the same fielder's glove. If I had some hits the night before, or if we won, or both, I'll wear the same gloves in batting practice the next night no matter how old or bad they are. I wear the same hat as long as I feel like we're playing good.

During batting practice, usually you'll use one fielder's glove that you're trying to break in, and you'll use your gamer during the game. Last year I went through a bunch of different gloves. I couldn't find one that really felt right. Usually I'll pack two gloves to go on the road. Last year I took a bunch, every different glove they ever made. So if I used, say, a Wilson glove in batting practice and a Mizuno in the game, I'd do the same thing the next night. I'd just feel funny if I changed.

I have a thing about my socks, too. I don't wear the regular baseball stirrup socks because I wear my pants so low. I have two or three different pairs at any given time. Sometimes they put your number on the top, sometimes on the bottom. If we're winning or we won the night before, I'll try to remember which socks I wore and how I pulled them on. And if we lose, maybe I'll switch and put the second pair on first. I know it's silly, but that's the way it is.

But that's about it.

Except for the bubble gum. Now, I start the game with four pieces of bubble gum. If things are going pretty good, I'll keep those in and add four more at the end of the inning. If things aren't going our way, I'll spit them out and start over.

My record is probably forty pieces. At once. But, see, when you chew it and the sugar gets out of it, the wad gets real small. So it's not as bad as it sounds. But those extra inning games kill me. I can't eat anything after the game because my jaw hurts so bad.

That's all, though.

Well, okay, then there's the route to the ballpark. I have been known to change routes to try to change our luck, even if I wasn't exactly sure where I was going. One time I got into a habit where I would get on that bridge that leads to the stadium and I'd drive past Veterans Stadium and I'd curse at it. Don't ask me why. Right before I got off at the exit I'd start screaming at the stadium. "You bastard! You son of a bitch! I'm going to kick your ass today!" Stuff like that. It didn't make any sense and I'm sure if anybody driving past me saw me, they thought I was nuts. But I was in a slump the first time I did it, and I got two or three hits that day. So of course I had to keep doing it. Nobody in the car but me and I'm driving along and cursing at the stadium for no apparent reason.

And you can't take your helmet for granted, either. The thing is, I don't use a new pair of batting gloves every day. Some players do, but if I get a pair that feels good, unless they rip I'll keep using them. So the pine tar starts building up, and then when I touch my helmet, it starts getting on there. Sometimes, like if it's raining, I'll put a little more pine tar up there so I can just touch the helmet if I need to get a little more stickum on my hands.

After the All-Star game the front office started getting calls from people saying my helmet was ugly because of all the pine tar and it needed to be cleaned. So I cleaned it. But I wasn't hitting that well after that, so I made a conscious decision that I wasn't going to do that anymore.

By the end of the season, it looked beautiful again.

Look at Mariano Duncan's uniform. He doesn't touch his helmet, but he uses a lot of pine tar on his bat, so from swinging and holding the bat down low, he has big brown stripes on his uniform. What are they going to do, make him change into a clean uniform after every at bat?

They told me they wanted me to clean my batting helmet because they couldn't see the team logo. Now, how tough is it to figure out who I play for? If you lose that *P* on the batting helmet, the big "Phillies" across my chest might just give it away.

The batboys clean the helmets before every game, but I told them just to leave mine be. I guess you could call it superstitious. I just don't like a clean helmet. And, if you'll notice, after I went back to dirtying it up and I started hitting again, nobody said a word.

Isn't it amazing? The better you play, the worse you can look.

When you're hitting, you don't think that much about superstitions. It's when you're making outs that you go up the tunnel and say, "It's the fuckin' helmet." There were times after I cleaned it that I would curse the helmet because I made an out. Which is silly. The helmet didn't swing the bat for me. But I'd walk past Jim Fregosi and I'd drop this subtle little hint that if he hadn't made me clean my damn helmet, I would have gotten a hit. Or if I can't wear my helmet the way I want, what the hell am I doing here? Stuff like that. Stuff you say when you're mad.

Of course, sometimes I've gotten a nice new shiny helmet and it didn't have anything to do with the front office. I've gone through five or six in a year, busting them when I made an out. You know, those things are hard to break. You'd think they wouldn't be, because they're just made of plastic, but there have been times when I've tried to shatter one with my bat, really hit it, and it wouldn't break. Then I'd really get pissed off because I would think my swing must really be bad if I can't break this little piece of plastic. No wonder I can't get a hit.

So I'm really pounding it until it breaks and then they get me a new one. And I have to wear a clean helmet for a while. But I don't like to do that, because it takes a lot of work to get a new helmet back to the way you want it, all scuffed up so you can get a good grip.

But like I said, I don't pay too much attention to that superstitious stuff. Except, of course, when I ripped my uniform pants in Game 6 of the playoffs. No way was I going to let them give me a new pair of pants.

And sometimes I'll try to remember to wear the same wristbands on the same arms. People think this stuff is easy, that all you have to do is go out and play. Everything is there for you. But they wash your stuff after every game and then you have to try to remember which wristband you wore where on the night you won and how you wore them the night you lost.

Then you have to remember to switch them around if you want to change your luck.

It's a trying experience, really.

And then there are the times you ask them not to wash your stuff. I've known some guys who wouldn't get their socks washed because we had won or they had a good game or something like that. I've told them to make sure to hang my T-shirt in the same spot as it was the night before. Different stuff like that. Or I tell them to make sure to pack my batting gloves, and maybe one day they'd tell me to pack them myself. I say, "No, you pack them. It worked better that way." You know, just idiosyncrasies.

But, no, I don't think I'm all that superstitious.

Or you might change the T-shirt you wear under your uniform. Some of them are clever. Some of them are nasty. I was wearing one for a while that Mitch Williams's dad gave me. It said something about how I've got a big tool, which probably isn't right.

Then there was one they gave me in San Diego. I don't know whether they had them made up especially for me or whether they saw it in a shop. It had a picture of a sheep and it said: "West Virginia. Where Men Are Men And Sheep Are Nervous." I wore that under my uniform for a long time, but when I got traded I got rid of it. I'd had it for so long that it was starting to smell not real good. I was wondering why nobody was talking to me anymore, then I gave it a little sniff under the arms and realized it had really started to stink, so I had to ditch it.

There are all kinds of superstitions in baseball. There's one that has been around the National League for years. The route from downtown Chicago to Wrigley Field goes past this big statue of a horse, and the rule is that the rookies have to go out and paint the horse's testicles your team color. I never had to do that because it seemed like we always followed the

Giants into Chicago; their team color was orange, same as San Diego's.

Then, when the bus passes, somebody yells, "Don't look at the horse's balls." Then you feel like a pervert for looking. But it's supposed to be bad luck if you do.

That's a rookie thing, just like the shoes in Atlanta. There's this store that sells shoes from the 1970s—I don't know quite how to describe them. It's like shoes that they're hoping will come back into style in thirty years. Platform shoes. The kind Elton John was wearing on the cover of the Yellow Brick Road album. The kind that, if you're five feet ten they make you look like you're six feet seven. I mean, they sell nice shoes there, too. All the players go in there. But they still have a bin full of these old shoes.

So you go in there and you figure out how many rookies are on your team. You get their sizes from their spikes, and you buy these shoes for all of them. Then you come in early one day with a bunch of markers and paints and put their number and a bunch of different stuff on them. Then, on getaway day, the pitchers steal their dress shoes during the game, and the rookies have to wear these big old ugly shoes on the team flight and into the next hotel.

Most guys go along with it. Once there were a couple guys who wouldn't do it, so they wore their turf shoes instead. Hell, that made them look even worse. They had on a nice suit and a pair of red baseball shoes. But for the most part they accept it and it's neat to watch them walking around on these high platform shoes with the flight attendants and everybody laughing at them. It's kind of neat to embarrass the rookies and put them in their place for a while.

Then there was the year Dave Hollins was a rookie. He was wise to the shoe bit so he packed an extra pair of dress shoes in his equipment bag. We couldn't get a good read on him at first. He's so big and strong that nobody wanted to piss him off, since he probably could have killed all of us if he wanted to. But then it was like, "The hell with him. He's a rookie." He had outsmarted us and we just couldn't let that happen.

So he got the deep freeze after that. When you're trying to play a joke on a rookie, you don't like to get fooled yourself. And he fooled us. He was a little smarter than we gave him credit for. We had to get him back. Finally, after a week or so, Dave volunteered to wear the shoes. I don't think he ever did, though; it was enough that he admitted he was wrong to trick us. The veterans are like Mother Nature. It's not nice to fool Mother Nature.

There are a couple other practical jokes that used to work well on rookies. One is the mongoose in Cincinnati. The clubhouse guys there have been pulling that one for years, since long before I started playing. They bring out a cage and tell the rookie that there's a dangerous mongoose inside. All you can see is a tail. They say he's asleep now but let's throw him some sunflower seeds and see if he'll wake up. They shake the cage and tap it. All the guys get around and sort of push the young guys to the front. And when they get right up close, the clubhouse guys hit something. The door flies open and the tail flies out and if you don't expect it, you go running.

It worked on me when I was a rookie. Scared the hell out of me.

There's another joke where one guy will say he's so strong that he can pick up five guys at once. Pete Incaviglia will say he can do it, and somebody bets that he can't. So you get five guys together. The rookie gets in the middle and the other four guys lay on his arms and legs. And then, when he can't move, you get him with shaving cream, ketchup, mustard, mayonnaise, Gatorade, whatever. Just pour it all over him and he's a mess when you're done.

When Roger McDowell was with us, he had this horn that looked kind of like a French horn, kind of curled around. He would tell a guy that it was a good-luck horn, and the louder the guy could blow the horn, the more luck we'd have. Well, you know how superstitious players are, so the guy wants to do what he can to help the team. So he blows the horn. It's filled with talcum powder. He blows it, and no sound comes out, just powder, and it goes all over his face.

The thing is, we can't play those tricks as much anymore. They've started to filter down to Triple-A. Even to the lower minor leagues. So when the kids come up, they're on to us. They're a little smarter than we give them credit for. So now that they're a little more advanced, I guess we'll have to think of some new tricks.

Players can also be superstitious about numbers. I should know, I've had a bunch of them.

In San Diego I was the last guy to wear number 44 before they retired it for Willie McCovey. He had played there a couple years. I was wearing it with the Padres, but when he was voted into the Hall of Fame, they retired it. That was kind of exciting. The next year I went back to number 8, which is what I had worn in the minors. I wore it for the rest of the time I was there. Then when I was traded to Philadelphia, they gave me number 11. Juan Samuel had number 8, and that was fine. I think the magic had kind of worn off it for me.

The next year I changed to number 19 because I was playing left field and the Phillies had had a pretty good Polish left fielder before me who wore that number—the Bull, Greg Luzinski.

Now, when you want to change your number, you have to go to the equipment man and beg and plead. They have all the jerseys made up and they like to keep it at that. But I really begged and pleaded and he let me have it. He wasn't really happy when I came back a year later and told him I wanted to switch again, to number 28.

I really don't know why. Tommy Herr had it before me. It

looked good. I hit behind him and I saw him on the bases. He was playing second base, and I had just moved to first base. It just looked like a good number.

Then we traded for Mitch Williams. He had worn number 28 in Texas and Chicago, and he wanted it. So I ended up taking number 29 and I've had it ever since.

Players can get attached to numbers. When Larry Bowa came to coach third base for the Phillies, he wanted number 10 because that's what he'd worn when he was a player here, but Darren Daulton had it. I never heard Bowa say it, but I think he felt like Darren was going through some lean years then and he wasn't living up to that number. Now that Darren has come into his own, I think Bowa accepts it.

It's funny, really; when you're playing, you can't see what number you're wearing. It's not like you can look down and say, "Oh, I'm number such-and-such. That's my favorite number, so I'm going to get a hit."

It's just a feeling. You may not think about it, really, but it's like an identity. When you think of Dave Winfield, you think of number 31. You think of Michael Jordan, you think of number 23. You think of Larry Bird, number 33.

In fact, I think the whole uniform can have an impact on the way you play. It's like putting on clothes. Your wife buys you an outfit and you think, "My God, this isn't pretty." But you don't tell her and you just wear it. That's kind of the same way it is when they give you a uniform. There's not much you can do about it. They got it for you, so you have to wear it.

I've worn some hideous uniforms in my life.

The Padres road uniforms were probably the ugliest of them all. Nobody was sure what color they really were. I thought they were light brown with a dark brown pinstripe, which made for ugly. They had an orange and dark brown SD on the chest and a dark brown hat. It looked like we had been out playing in the dirt all day and then came out and decided to play a ball game in the same clothes.

The uniforms we wore in Beaumont weren't real attractive, either. The Golden Gators. Old-time crown hats, green, with a big gold band around them. Green stars in the gold band. Gold bills. Green uniforms with large gold stripes all down the side, and green stars. And a big green alligator topping it all off.

I think I know what Mr. Blackwell would have thought.

The thing is, every time you go out wearing an ugly uniform, you know you're wearing ugly. At first people would say things. After a while, though, they just accepted that it was ugly and let it alone.

Every other uniform I wore in the minors, except at Triple-A, was a hand-me-down from the big league team. They were regular uniforms though. The Las Vegas uniforms were kind of different—white with an orange and brown stripe down the side and the word "Stars" across the chest with stars and stripes all around it. They were kind of flashy and Vegasy. But they weren't nearly as bad as those Padres road uniforms. I was almost embarrassed to go on the road. I mean, you can look at me and realize that I'm no fashion genius, but I don't think anyone could take those colors and mix them together and make them look good.

Those players who have only been in San Diego the last couple years, since they changed, don't realize how lucky they are.

When we first heard that the Phillies were getting new uniforms a couple years ago, I was a little concerned. We didn't have any idea what they were going to look like. Those old blue road uniforms with the zipper in front weren't real pretty. The new ones turned out nice, though.

The biggest problem was that the front office kept them such a big secret that we didn't get them until opening day. They looked nice, but we had a lot of problems with the crotch area. I think they made the uniforms for people without a crotch. I'm trying to say this nicely. Like for a women's softball team, you know? Everybody was switching and trading and trying to find something that would work. By the time the game started, we just went out there with what we had and hoped that, win or lose, everybody made it through without getting ruptured.

As long as a uniform fits, I don't really worry about how I look when I'm playing. But something as ugly as those Padres road uniforms is really depressing. I know I didn't feel too good wearing them.

Then again, the Twins won the world championship in 1987 and 1991 and their uniforms were pretty ugly. And we won the championship with those awful uniforms in Beaumont. If you can win with those, you can win with anything.

So none of that stuff has anything to do with winning. It's all just superstition. But I still think I'll keep track of my socks and wristbands and T-shirts. There's no sense taking a chance, is there?

We felt like every game, we were going to win. We were surprised when we didn't.

EVERY YEAR YOU COME TO SPRING training and reporters ask, "What do you think your chances will be this season?" And every year you say, "Well, if we don't have too many injuries and we play up to our potential, we have as good a chance as anybody." Same old shit. Sometimes we even tell ourselves that.

A lot of times, though, we know it really isn't true.

Last year we went to Clearwater and we said the usual things. This time, though, we honestly believed it. Just from the way everybody got along right from the beginning, it was like we all clicked.

It really hit me after one of the early exhibition games. We had played somewhere on the road, maybe against the Reds in Plant City. Usually you come back after a game like that and everybody just takes a shower and goes out to dinner or whatever. But this day it didn't happen. I don't know why. We just sat around the clubhouse, talking, almost every guy on the team. Somebody sent out for a couple cases of beer. We called our wives and said we'd be late for dinner. We just sat and talked for hours.

Then when I left, when I got back home, it hit me: *We have a really good team. We're going to win a lot of games. We're going to be in the race.*

Jim Fregosi did a good job of keeping that feeling going. Usually he couldn't care less about winning games in Florida, but this year it was different.

We knew we had to get off to a good start in the regular season; Phillies teams in the last few years had a habit of getting buried early. You talk about what a long season it is and how there's no reason you can't turn things around, but the truth is, it's tough if you're already six or seven games out by the end of April. We wanted to avoid that, and playing harder in the spring was a part of it.

It wasn't that we played every game like it was the seventh game of the World Series or anything like that. Guys got their work and guys got their rest. Pitchers got their innings. But Fregosi put a little more emphasis on winning. We finished up with a decent record, and that gave us a little more confidence going into the season.

Before last season maybe we went into a game thinking

about how we could win. But then after a while we went into every game saying, "How could these guys beat us?" We felt like we were going to win every game. We were surprised when we didn't.

And the perfect thing happened to us to start the season.

We started out in Houston. Normally that wouldn't be a good thing; the Astros are always tough at home, and they had gone out and signed two of the best pitchers in the league as free agents, Doug Drabek and Greg Swindell. They were both Texans. The team also had a new owner who had everybody pretty excited. There were going to be big crowds rooting against us. The Astros figured to be tougher than ever.

We won three straight.

Curt Schilling had said in the newspaper during spring training that our starting pitching could be as good as anybody's. As good as the Braves. Pitching still had a chance to be our Achilles' heel, though. So when Terry Mulholland went in there to start the season and pitched a complete game four-hitter, giving up one unearned run, it couldn't have been a better way to open. We beat Drabek, 3–1.

The next night we faced Swindell. Schilling pitched into the ninth and we won again. Mitch Williams got the save.

At that point, it would have been easy to say, well, this has been a success no matter what; even if we lose the last game of the series, we've still taken two out of three and we're off to a great start. After six innings it would have been *real* easy to say that. Pete Harnisch was pitching a no-hitter against us.

But Darren Daulton led off the seventh with a home run. Harnisch left the game for a pinch-hitter in the bottom of the inning. We scored twice in the eighth to tie it up and won it with three in the tenth. Danny Jackson, who we got in a trade to strengthen the rotation, did exactly what we had hoped he would do, pitching seven strong innings. Mitch got his second save.

Everybody was more sure than ever that this was going to be a big year.

After that, everything just seemed to fall into place. If we needed a big hit, we got it. If we needed a well-pitched game, we got it. If we needed a big play in the field, same thing. And it wasn't the same guys night after night.

About ten days later we were in Chicago. Wrigley Field. Wind blowin' out. We were ahead, 4–0, going into the bottom of the seventh. We were ahead, 8–4, going into the bottom of the eighth. We were ahead, 11–8, going into the bottom of the eleventh. Wound up winning, 11–10. David West came in with one out and a runner on first and got a double-play grounder to end the game.

On April 26 at the Vet, we were playing the Giants. Going into the bottom of the sixth, we were behind, 8–0. But we scored three in the sixth, four in the seventh, one in the eighth, and one in the tenth when Juan Bell scored from third on a wild pitch. The Fightin' Phils won again.

I never thought we were out of it. You don't necessarily think about coming back and winning a game like that, but you know you're going to get some guys on base and you know you're going to score some runs. It's just a matter of getting enough guys on base and bringing them in. It's a matter of getting key hits. And that's the way the season went. We got key hits all year long.

This was really getting to be fun. We were starting to attract a lot of attention from the national media. They were all coming in to do the story about how wild we were. I don't know where they got that idea. Just because the Spin Doctors were always blasting from the CD player and guys were running around throwing pies in each other's faces and yelling insults at each other. But we were just having fun.

Coming out of spring training, another thing people questioned about our team was the defense. We probably didn't play as well on defense as we could have or should have, but a lot of times we made the play when we had to.

Like in San Diego on April 29. We were leading, 5–3, in the bottom of the ninth, but the Padres had the bases loaded with two outs. Their catcher, Bob Geren, hit a long drive to left center that would have been a grand slam, except that Milt Thompson jumped and caught the ball to keep it from going over.

The very next night we're playing the Dodgers in Los Angeles. We're ahead, 7–6, in the bottom of the ninth. But Mitch is in trouble. There's already one run in. The bases are loaded, and there's nobody out. Mike Sharperson was the pinch-hitter, and he hit a bullet up the middle. Tommy Lasorda, the Dodgers manager, started clapping and running out of the dugout to celebrate. He thought it was a two-run single and they had won the game.

But Mickey Morandini, our second baseman, dove to his right and somehow caught the ball in the air. He crawled over and tagged second to double off the runner. Eric Davis, who was at third, had to get back. Then Mitch got Brett Butler to ground into a fielder's choice and we had won again.

That's one reason I think Mickey is a big part of our team. There aren't too many second basemen who make that play. Roberto Alomar and Chico Lind, maybe, but they're both in the other league. That's about it. As far as range and everything else goes, I can't think of a better second baseman in our league.

We needed that defense, too. Once Kevin Stocker came up and started playing shortstop, it helped; Dave Hollins at third and I could just tell ourselves, "Step and dive and let those two guys take care of the rest."

Another big win came on May 9, against the Cardinals back at the Vet. We were behind, 5–2, going into the bottom of the eighth. We hadn't done zip against Bob Tewksbury. There were two outs and nobody on.

Then Darren Daulton singled. Wes Chamberlain doubled to put runners on second and third. Lee Smith came in to face Milt Thompson, who walked to load the bases. And Mariano Duncan hit a grand slam to win the game. We were 22–7 and had a six-and-a-half-game lead over the Expos, who were in second place at the time. Instead of getting buried early, we were doing a little digging of our own.

The next night against the Pirates, it was Darren's turn to win the game with a grand slam. This one came in the seventh.

Right after that we made our first trip of the season into Atlanta. The press made a big deal out of it; after all, we had the best record in baseball and the Braves were considered the best team in the league, at least, going into the season. There was a lot of talk about how it was an important series.

Well, there's no such thing as a crucial series in May. We were still going to have fun. We traveled on the off-day before the series opened. Terry Mulholland and Mark Davis went to the Underground and bought T-shirts, one for every guy on the team. They all had something on them that had something to do with the guy who got them. Let's just say mine had to do with drinking beer. About the only one that's printable was Tommy Greene's: it said something like "Six weeks ago I couldn't spell gradewate and now I are one."

We ended up losing two out of three, but they were all good games. We had our chances to win each one. We left Atlanta with a 25–10 record and a four-and-a-half-game lead over Montreal and flew to Florida still feeling pretty good about ourselves.

One of the longest and weirdest days of the season came about six weeks later, on July 2. At least it started on July 2. We had a doubleheader scheduled against the Padres. There were three rain delays lasting nearly six hours. We lost the first

game. By the time it ended, it was after midnight, but it wasn't
raining anymore, so we just went ahead and started the second
game.

The Padres scored twice in the top of the fourth to take a
5–0 lead. Andy Benes was pitching for San Diego. He was only
leading the league in earned run average at the time. So we
were way behind against a real good pitcher. It was the middle
of the night. There was almost nobody in the stands. It would
have been a perfect time to fold it up, get some rest, and go get
them the next day. I mean, later that day.

But we scored a run in the bottom of the fourth, and Ricky
Jordan hit a three-run homer in the fifth. We tied it up in the
eighth. We thought we had it won in the ninth when we had
runners on second and third, but then their pitcher bounced
one. We were kind of out of players by then, so Tommy
Greene, a pitcher, was the pinch-runner at third. He tried to
score, but their catcher, Kevin Higgins, hustled after the ball
and threw to the plate, and Greenie was out.

The home plate umpire, Larry Poncino, made the call.
"You're out! Dammit! You're out."

I didn't know whether to laugh or cry. There was only one
way for that game to end properly, and it did: Mitch Williams
singled Pete Incaviglia home with the winning run at 4:40 in
the morning.

Is it any wonder we began to believe that this was meant to
be?

One thing about Ricky Jordan: if you can only count on the
eight guys who play every day to win, you're not going to do
it. You're going to have to bring guys off the bench. It's a
shame that Ricky had to sit so much because he's a damn good
hitter. He'll get his chance and he deserves it. He's more than
paid his dues. He's got credit on his balance due.

That's one thing I don't like about baseball. Here's a guy
playing the same position I do. He's got a lot of talent. He's

not getting to play that much. You know, he could have gone home at night and said, "That fat bastard . . ." But I've never heard him say anything bad about me. That shows a lot of class. I know he was chomping at the bit to play. I don't think there are many people who would have handled it as well as he did.

Of course, if it's some idiot I can't stand sitting behind me, to hell with him.

Anyway, a couple days after that game, we qualified for overtime again. Lenny Dykstra homered to lead off the sixth, putting us ahead of the Dodgers, 5–3, at the Vet. In the next ten innings, we got exactly two hits. The Dodgers had tied the score meanwhile and we played and played and played. When they scored in the top of the twentieth, they had to figure we were beaten. Wrong again. Lenny doubled two runs home in the bottom of the twentieth and we won, 7–6.

That was Kevin Stocker's first game in the majors. He had to be wondering what he was getting into.

We were playing great. Everything was breaking our way. But I think we all knew, down deep, that it couldn't go that well all season. Baseball just doesn't work that way. We found out we were right and we found out sooner than we thought.

The next team into town was the Giants, for the last four games before the All-Star break. They beat us in the first game, 13–2. They beat us in the second game, 15–8. They beat us in the last game, 10–2. We managed to sneak one win in there. I'm not quite sure how.

That was the only time during the whole season when we got behind early and we really didn't think we had a chance to come back. They hit bombs. They hit rocket line drives into the gap. Then they blooped one in. You know, tip your hat; they just came in and waxed our ass. It was like, "Man, we ain't going to win." I didn't think we were going to score, and I didn't think they could stop scoring. In some of those games, they were almost scoring by accident—they didn't want to, but they couldn't help it.

What made it worse was that we had been getting such good pitching for the first couple months of the season. And then it was like Tommy Greene and Curt Schilling forgot how to pitch for a while. I don't know why. They both have overpowering stuff. I don't think they realize how hard it is to hit a good fastball in a good spot.

A couple of weeks earlier Schilling had come out with that statement about how he had lost his confidence. I think that's when he gets in trouble, when he talks too much. He wants to be everyone's friend, and if reporters give him the chance, he'll fill up their notebooks. But there are just some things he shouldn't say.

We had a long talk with him—me and Darren Daulton and Larry Andersen. I think Jim Eisenreich was there, too. We told him, "How can you not have confidence with that kind of arm? You see a guy throwing eighty miles an hour and he's not hitting his spots, fine. But with the kind of fastball you've got, you can miss your spots and still get away with it."

I don't think he realized that. He's no Bob Tewksbury. Tewksbury throws harder than most people think, but still, if he's not putting the ball where he wants it with all his pitches, he could be in a little trouble. But when you have a fastball like Schilling's, when in doubt, you rely on old number one. At least, that's what I was always told. If you're struggling, go with your best pitch. Don't be half-assed.

It came to a head with Schilling after a game in St. Louis on July 1, the getaway day of a four-game series. We had lost two out of three, but if we won this game we would split and not lose ground. But Schilling gave up eleven runs, seven earned, in two and two-thirds innings, and we got killed. And coming after his comments about losing confidence, how the hell are we supposed to go to war behind him after that? That day in

St. Louis we felt he had quit on us and it really pissed a bunch of us off.

Darren kind of got on him in the newspaper. He told the writers it was the most embarrassing game he'd ever been associated with. He said he didn't know if Schill was "tired, nervous, scared, worried, feeling the pressure, whatever." Normally we don't like to do things through the press, but this time Darren thought it was necessary.

When we got back to Philadelphia we had another meeting, this time with the whole team. We had lost five out of six. Two weeks earlier we had been ahead by eleven and a half games. Now it was down to five and a half. Schilling got blistered pretty good by a lot of us. He might not think that helped him, but it helped us to just tell him how we felt, that he was pitching like a pussy and some other things. And after that he kicked it back in and pitched good the rest of the way.

We talked to Tommy Greene, too, but he's a different case. Here's a guy who throws 95 miles an hour but he always feels like he's throwing 60. He doesn't realize what kind of stuff he has. I've had guys come down to first and say, "How's this guy ever lose? His stuff is electric."

Anyway, for a while there, we were struggling. On June 25 we were 51–21. We were nine and a half games ahead of St. Louis and thirteen games up on Montreal. From then until the All-Star break we went 6–11. St. Louis was within five. Then we lost three in a row after the break. Our lead was down to three.

I don't think we ever panicked, though. We were kind of like a young player who starts out good and then rests on his laurels. I think that's what we did. We got away from the things we did when we were getting off to that good start. In that stretch, we didn't score that many runs, and our pitching wasn't that good, either. And then we started thinking about the year before. Oh, no, here we go again. Our pitching can't hold them. And when they do pitch good, we don't score. And when we score a lot, the pitchers can't get anyone out.

You heard it around the clubhouse: "Our pitchers suck. How many runs do we have to score?" And I'm sure our pitchers were saying, "If those guys had just caught that ball" or "If we had just gotten a hit there we would have been ahead and it would have been a different game." That's another good reason to keep hitters and pitchers a little separate from each other.

If there had been another month to go before the All-Star break, it could have been a bad scene if we'd kept playing like that and acting like that.

But thank God for three days off. We just needed to get away from each other. Playing on a team is like being married, we're around each other so much. It was good to get away, regroup, come back, and start playing better. And that's what we did.

Darren Daulton and I were elected to start in the All-Star game. I told the media it was a big honor to be voted in by the fans. It's a chance to play against the best players in the world, and this meant that the fans thought we were two of the best. And that says a lot about what's wrong with society today.

I got a letter from Bill White, the National League president, congratulating me. It was the first time I'd ever gotten a letter from him that wasn't asking me to pay a fine, the first one that didn't start out, "Please make check payable to . . ."

Dave Hollins and Terry Mulholland also made the All-Star team. Terry at first said he didn't want to go, that he'd rather spend the time at home in Arizona. Did I mention that he's a pitcher? Anyway, we ended up talking him into it and he was the National League starter.

If anybody still remembers that All-Star game a hundred years from now, they're probably going to remember my at bat against Randy Johnson. It must have been quite a sight:

tall and skinny, short and fat, Mutt and Jeff. And then he throws the first pitch over my head. I mean, it's supposed to be fun. You want to win. You want to do well. But you also don't want to get hurt and screw up the rest of your season.

Darren and I had gone on ESPN with Roy Firestone the day of the All-Star workout. Firestone asked me about facing Johnson, and I said there was no way. And, lo and behold, I think Cito Gaston was listening. He was like a nightmare all season long. First he managed the American League All-Stars and put Randy Johnson in when I was coming up, and then he managed Toronto against us in the World Series.

That at bat was going to be the same no matter where that first pitch went. I just wasn't real enthusiastic about being in there. Let's just say I wasn't thinking about digging in and hanging tough.

Have you ever done something when you were younger, like break into a barn or something? Now here comes the guy with his gun. But you don't run straight. You zigzag. That's the way I felt. If Johnson was going to hit me, it wasn't going to be because I was stationary.

It would have been embarrassing to die on national TV. Besides, you can't hit good when you're dead.

After that first pitch, I just said, "Here, the plate is yours. Go ahead and take it." And he did. I was bailing out like a little kid. I was never so happy to strike out in my life. The thing is, he threw two pretty good breaking balls right after that, and that ain't fair. I wasn't too upset to see him sign that long-term contract with Seattle. They could keep him up in the Northwest. I didn't want to see that guy again. He's frightening. I knew one thing: if he got traded to the National League, Fregosi wouldn't ever play me against him again.

It's not that Johnson throws so hard that scares you. The only time you're really scared is when you're not picking up the ball out of the guy's hand. That's scary. That's when you can get hurt. I wouldn't want to see any of our other guys go up against him, either. In his very next start, he hit a guy in the head with a pitch. Some people didn't like my at bat against him. They said, "Aw, he's just joking around," about that pitch over my head. But after that next start I had my doubts.

The Randy Johnson experience was my third All-Star game. I didn't get to play in the first one, in Toronto, but it was an honor just to be picked.

The second game was fun because it was back in San Diego. The first couple times I had been back as a Phillie they cheered me. After that they booed me. I didn't know what to expect at the All-Star game, but I got a real nice ovation and I got a hit off Jeff Montgomery, who had played college ball at Marshall University in West Virginia.

That was fun because, during the workout the day before, Jeff came over to me and said he wanted to get his picture taken with me—fellow West Virginians. Then I had to face him in my first at bat as an All-Star and I got a hit. It was kind of exciting.

That was also the year we didn't have a shirt to wear for the workout. We had just finished playing the Padres to close out the first half of the season, so our equipment should have been right there, but they had taken the game shirts to get the All-Star patch sewn on and we didn't have anything to wear.

We tried sending somebody up to the concession stand, Darren and I, to see if they could buy any kind of a Phillies shirt, but they didn't have any. The lady said they didn't carry Phillies stuff. I told Darren, "We must really suck if you can't buy any kind of Phillies shirt at the All-Star game."

I borrowed a Braves shirt from Leo Mazzone. I've signed a lot of pictures that were taken of me wearing his shirt. Leo has one in his locker.

Anyway, the All-Star break came at just the right time for

us last year. It was time to get back to business. When we got
back to Philadelphia, everyone was focused: Nice seeing you
guys again, let's start playing ball like we played earlier. The
Giants series is over. We took our pounding; let's dust ourselves off, get up like men, and start playing good.

St. Louis made a little run at us, but they came to our place
at the end of July, and we swept them in a three-game series.
That was something that had to be done. When we were at
Busch Stadium a month earlier they beat us pretty handy. Well,
tip your hat to them. But then we read some of the stuff their
players were saying about us. *If they don't think they're in a
race now, they've got another think coming. We're right on
their heels*. That sort of stuff.

And, you know, I think their comments added a little incen-
tive when we played them. You don't like to hear stuff like
that. When the game got serious, we had a little more heart,
and we did the job. After we swept them we were in the clubhouse before the media came in, and Darren told everyone,
"Keep your mouth shut. Let's go about our business. If the
Cardinals want to keep chirping, let them keep chirping. But
we did our job and that's all that matters. We don't need to
brag about it. It's done. It's over. Now let's go on to the next
series."

One thing about our team, we didn't go out and talk trash
about other teams. We're known for trash talking, but just
among ourselves. I don't ever remember anybody saying something derogatory about the other team. That's foolish. You
look at how hard you had to work to get there, and you know
the other guys worked just as hard. We're all in the same boat.
I respect everyone who puts on a uniform, because they know
what it takes to get here. It isn't easy. So I ain't gonna talk
trash about another team.

But we didn't have it won yet. Montreal got hot. They put
a little run together. Little run? On August 20, they lost to the

Reds and were in third place, fourteen and a half games out. Then they won twenty of their next twenty-three and were only five games out when we went in there to play them.

You don't expect any team to have a streak like that, not even the 1927 Yankees. Not anybody. But the Expos kept winning and we kept watching. And they kept winning and we kept watching. After a while, it was, "Holy shit, they have to lose once in a while. Don't they?"

We played them at Olympic Stadium, three games in the middle of September. All three games were decided by one run. It was absolute pressure, and even though we didn't really do what we wanted to do, those games helped prepare us for the playoffs. It was a helluva series.

Montreal won the first game, 8–7, in twelve innings, to get the lead down to four. Ben Rivera started for us and was knocked out of the game in the fifth. We batted around in the sixth, scored seven runs, and knocked Dennis Martinez out of the game. The Expos came back and scored once against Bobby Thigpen in the sixth and three more in the seventh to tie the score.

Mitch Williams got through the eleventh inning without giving up a run even though he walked a couple guys with one out. But in the twelfth, Marquis Grissom led off with a double, stole third, and scored on Delino DeShields's sacrifice fly. And that was it.

The next night, over fifty thousand came out for the game. That was partly because the Expos were in the pennant race and partly because their starting pitcher, Dennis Boucher, was a Canadian. He was a real favorite.

The fans didn't have much to cheer about, though, until the bottom of the eighth. By then Boucher was gone and we had a 5–1 lead. Tommy Greene only gave up two hits in the first seven innings, but Sean Berry led off the eighth with a single and John Vander Wal, a pinch-hitter, got a base hit, too. Wil

Cordero homered. Now it was a one-run game, and Jim Fregosi brought David West out of the bullpen.

He retired the side. Mitch came in to pitch the ninth. With one out, he walked Larry Walker. Then he threw the ball away trying to pick him off. What was even worse, when I went over to pick up the ball I stepped on it and just about blew out my knee and back. It was scary because Walker was getting into scoring position. And it was embarrassing. I'm not sure what the crowd was saying then, but I think it was French for "Here's this big fatass rolling around on the field for no reason." Then Walker stole third. He was ninety feet away from tying the game and there was still only one out.

But we ended up winning the game, so everyone had a pretty good laugh at my troubles. Mitch got the job done. He struck out Mike Lansing, the pinch-hitter, then he got Berry to fly out. It was Mitch's thirty-ninth save, and our lead was back to five.

In the final game we had a one-run lead going into the bottom of the ninth, but we ended up losing. And it was partly my fault.

Mitch was pitching again and there was one out. Then DeShields singled and stole second. Rondell White walked. And then it happened.

Larry Walker hit a grounder to me and I didn't field it cleanly. When I did get hold of the ball, I looked to see if we could get the force at second. We couldn't, so I turned and threw to Mitch who was covering first. Walker went into the base with a headfirst dive, and I thought he was out. But Charlie Williams, the umpire at first, called him safe.

There was no excuse for me bobbling the ball. But I still say we got the runner.

Mitch got Sean Berry to pop out for what should have been the last out of the game. Then Wil Cordero singled to score two runs and the Expos won. But we still had a four-game lead with only thirteen games left to play.

When we got the magic number down to about four, a sense of urgency set in. We started smelling it. It's like you've ordered a new car and you can't wait for it to come in so you can drive it. We couldn't wait to get to the ballpark.

We beat the Pirates at Three Rivers Stadium, 10–7, on September 28 to clinch the National League East championship. Dave Clark grounded out to me for the last out. I flipped to Donn Pall, the pitcher, covering. He had just joined us in September. He didn't look like he knew what to do. I grabbed him, and then the party started. Harry Kalas was singing. Todd Pratt was dancing—that was something to see; he's a large man. We went back to the hotel and we partied some more. It was a night I'll never forget.

There were still five games left in the regular season. It gave us a chance to set up our rotation and get Darren Daulton some rest. He needed it; he'd played something like twenty-five or thirty straight games. He's a horse, but even horses can wear down.

At that point we still didn't know whether we'd be playing San Francisco or Atlanta. That went right down to the last day of the season before the Braves won the NL West for the third straight year. They had to win 104 games to beat the Giants by one game.

We ended the regular season in St. Louis on Sunday, and then we had two days off before the playoffs started at the Vet. What a great series we had with Atlanta. It was like two boxers. They'd give us a good shot, then we'd give them a good shot. Back and forth.

The opener was like a fairy tale. We had a 3–2 lead going into the ninth, and then Kim Batiste, who was in the game as a defensive replacement at third base, fielded what could have been a double play grounder and threw it into right field. The Braves ended up tying the game on an unearned run, and we had to go into extra innings.

Mitch Williams left runners in scoring position in the top of the tenth. Then Batty comes up with one out and a runner on second in the bottom of the inning and singles in the winning run. Man, we were happy for him. I wouldn't have wanted to be in the situation he was in. He was real upset about making that error, but I've never seen a man smile so much as he did after he got that hit. But that was the way the whole season went: if somebody made a mistake, somebody else picked him up.

Game 2, we got killed, 14–3. The game was over by the third inning when Atlanta scored six runs. Fred McGriff hit a home run into the upper deck in right. The playoffs were tied at one game apiece when we went to Atlanta.

They beat us pretty good, 9–4, in Game 3. Terry Mulholland shut them out for five innings, but faced only five batters in the sixth and didn't get any of them out. Terry had a strained hip flexor that kept him from pitching much in September. He gave it all he had for five innings, but that was it.

Now we were facing our most important game of the season. Danny Jackson started and pitched his ass off. He held the Braves to one run in seven and two-thirds innings. Mitch Williams got the last four outs. We didn't do much better against John Smoltz, but we took advantage of an error to score two unearned runs in the fourth. That was all the scoring we did, but we won, 2–1.

We won our third playoff game by one run in Game 5 and our second in extra innings. Everything went our way. Curt Schilling pitched a great game. He also got one break. With two outs and Jeff Blauser on second in the bottom of the first, Fred McGriff hit a shot to right. Off the bat, I thought it was a two-run homer and who knows what would have happened after that, but the ball hit off the top of the fence, maybe a foot from being a homer. And Wes Chamberlain played the ball perfectly and made a great throw to the cutoff man, Kevin

Stocker, who made a perfect relay throw to the plate. Blauser was out, and Schill was out of the inning.

We managed to get one run against Steve Avery in the first inning and one more in the fourth. Darren Daulton led off the ninth with a home run off Greg McMichael. We were ahead, 3–0, and three outs away from leading the playoffs three games to two.

We didn't do too many things the easy way last year, and that game was no exception.

Schill walked Blauser to lead off the ninth. Then it happened again: Ron Gant hit a grounder to Kim Batiste, and Kim made another error. Now the Braves had runners on first and second with nobody out and Mitch came in from the bullpen.

Fred McGriff singled. Blauser scored, and Gant went to third. David Justice hit a sacrifice fly to left. Our lead was down to one. Terry Pendleton and pinch-hitter Francisco Cabrera singled. The score was tied, and Pendleton, the potential winning run, was on third.

Mark Lemke was up, and he smoked a line drive down the left field line. I thought that was it. Game over. That could have broken our hearts right there, but the ball went foul— barely—and Mitch struck Lemke out. Then Bill Pecota flied out, and we found ourselves in the tenth inning. Again.

Like he did so many times in the postseason, Lenny Dykstra came through. With one out, he homered to right off Mark Wohlers. Larry Andersen got the Braves out in order in the bottom of the inning, and we were one win away from going to the World Series.

All year we had thought we were unbeatable, and we approached the playoffs with the same attitude. And this time we were right. We scored six runs in Game 6 off Greg Maddux, who had only won the Cy Young Award. We might have gotten a break in the first inning, when Mickey Morandini hit a shot off Maddux's shin. Mickey was out and Maddux stayed in the game, but he wasn't quite as sharp as usual. Tommy Greene made up for Game 2 when he gave up seven runs in two and two-thirds innings. He pitched great.

David West stuffed the Braves in the eighth. Mitch Williams retired Atlanta in order in the ninth. And Veterans Stadium erupted. I think I had the most fun just running around the field. At least I did until I got hit in the back of the head by a television camera.

We celebrated in the clubhouse for a while. That was a blast. Todd Pratt danced again. Lenny Dykstra just went over and lay down in the corner of the training room for two or three hours, with his spikes still on, while the rest of us sprayed a lot of champagne. Everything comes out at a time like that—all your feelings toward your teammates, how you feel about everything and everyone. You can't think there could be anything better in life.

Mitch had gotten his second save of the playoffs. When he struck out Bill Pecota to end the game, he jumped higher than I thought a man could jump. He had taken a lot of crap during the season. Now he was grinning like an idiot.

None of us could have guessed that what was about to happen would change everything for Mitch.

**They say you're only young once,
but you can always be immature.
That's Mitch.**

THE FIRST TIME I MET MITCH WILLIAMS, HE was seventeen years old. We were both minor leaguers in the Padres organization. And what you have to understand is he hasn't changed since then. Back then he was this kid walking around with a little strut and tattoos on his calf. Now he makes three million dollars a year, and the only difference is he's got more tattoos. Other than that, same guy.

Mitch has a good heart. He means well. It's just that sometimes he's wrapped a little too tight. So I really didn't like seeing what was done to him after he blew a couple saves in the World Series, including giving up the home run to Joe Carter that won it for Toronto.

Mitch and I were drafted about a year apart. By the time I got to Triple-A he was in his second or third year in A ball. We were playing an exhibition game in Las Vegas against the Padres Class A Reno team. He came in to pitch. Bruce Bochy was the catcher; he told me later he'd caught Nolan Ryan and Goose Gossage, and this kid threw harder than either of them.

Now, I don't know if it was just a hot day in Vegas or Bochy was just under the weather or what.

But Mitch threw real hard then. I know; I got into the batting cage against him once in spring training. The first pitch he threw was out of the cage on the other side. The next pitch hit the bar on top of the cage and came bouncing down. The third pitch missed the cage entirely. The manager told me to get out of there before I got killed.

I didn't argue.

I never played on a team with him in the minor leagues, but I do remember hearing about the time his brother—I think his name was Bruce—was pitching in the Milwaukee Brewers system at Class A. Mitch was at Reno. They had a duel going to see who was going to lead the league in walks.

I think Mitch won.

That was about the time the Padres drafted Jimmy Jones in the first round. I remember Tom House, who was the pitching coach in Las Vegas then, telling me that he bet Mitch would win twice as many games in the big leagues as Jimmy Jones ever did, and that Mitch would pitch a lot longer. And then I watched him pitch in that exhibition game, and he threw the ball all over the place. I thought, maybe, but this guy has a lot of work to do.

I was glad I didn't have to hit against him.

I felt sorry for left-handed hitters like Tony Longmire and Bruce Dostal, young guys who had to take BP in the spring. Whenever Mitch had to throw, those were the only guys they would send up to hit—somebody had to stand in there, and it wasn't going to be a veteran. But you had to feel sorry for them. He could make you gun-shy.

At the same time, it wasn't as bad for them as it was for the guys who batted against Mitch earlier in his career. He threw harder back then—a whole lot harder. And his control is a lot better now, too.

People don't want to believe that, but it's true. He's Bob Tewksbury now compared to what he was then. When he got traded to Texas, I followed that wild act he threw out there. Then he got sent to the Cubs. A bunch of guys were saying, "The Cubs got rid of Lee Smith. That's got to be good."

I said, "Naw, it ain't good. You don't want to face this guy. You'd much rather face Lee Smith. 'Cause Lee Smith has got an idea where he's throwing the ball. And this guy has none."

Mitch proved me right.

He throws stuff all over. But he hides the ball so well and he falls off the mound; that makes him tough to hit, even if he doesn't throw as hard as he used to.

I'll tell you something else: he might have been the best natural athlete on our team. If he really worked at it, he could have been one of our best defensive outfielders, too. He might even have been one of our better hitters. I mean, if you put us all in a room and gave us a sport and said, "Go out and play this," he'd probably pick it up quicker than any of us. Over the long haul, somebody else in that room might learn to play the sport better, but at the beginning, Mitch would probably be the best.

When he pitched for the Cubs, you'd have to face him throwing out of those shadows in the late afternoon at Wrigley

Field. But he only came close to me once or twice. Even then, he was probably trying to throw low and away. You just never knew.

That's just Mitch. He hasn't changed. Oh, he might have gotten a little carried away about wearing number 99 like that guy in the movie *Major League*. But that's just the way Mitch is. He's just a big kid. I think in the last couple years he might have gotten a little hardened, though. He even came up to me one time and said, "You've got to stop saying those things about me in the paper. People are starting to believe them."

That might have been after he blew a save opportunity and we ended up playing twenty innings. I can't remember for sure, but I think I'd told a reporter, "I wanted to kill Mitch, but they told me I couldn't because it was illegal."

I think everything that happened to him at the end, all the death threats and stuff, might have made him grow up a little. I think he'll do a good job for Houston. I hope he doesn't pitch against us. I remember last year after we released Mark Davis; he signed with San Diego and pitched against us and stuck it up our butts.

Sure, Mitch would drive you crazy out there. They always say the worst thing a relief pitcher can do is come in and walk the first guy. But it was different for Mitch. *He* was different. I don't think he was intentionally wild. I don't think he consciously went out there and tried to throw balls into the dirt or to airmail them to the screen. It's just that sometimes he gets out of whack. Take when he struck out Bill Pecota and we won the playoffs; the pitch before, he'd bounced one behind him. He wasn't *trying* to do that. That's just Mitch. What can you say?

One time in spring training Bill Giles, the owner of the Phillies, was walking up some steps. He had been giving Mitch a little grief. Mitch was in center field and threw the ball at Giles and missed him by a foot. That's pretty accurate. Maybe he should try pitching from center field.

He might be one of those guys who was put on this earth not to have any money. He'll show up at spring training with a new car. It's hard to tell what he'll show up with. I mean, look at that headband he wears. And I've seen him bring guns into the clubhouse. He's even shown up with puppy dogs. He's always got something going. It's like if you give a ten-year-old kid a lot of money, it's hard to tell what he'll show up with. With Mitch, it's toys and gadgets, mostly. He just hasn't grown up yet. He's different from the rest of us. But he's a good person.

I'm really not sure why people in Philadelphia didn't take to him. He could save ten games in a row, but if he blew the eleventh they were all over him. I mean, here's a guy who set a team record with forty-three saves. And he was getting booed all the time. People were always saying he should be traded.

Maybe it was because, before last year, we lost so much that when we had a lead in the ninth, people wanted a secure save. Sure, it would have been nice to be able to bring in Dennis Eckersley, who throws maybe one ball a month. Or Bryan Harvey from the Marlins. But we had Mitch. And that pretty much epitomized the way our whole team played. We didn't do things the easy way.

You just had to accept that, with Mitch, 1-2-3 innings were going to be a rarity. When they happened, we were in a little bit of shock. But he was the guy we had to finish games for us, and we had to live with it. He helped us win the pennant. That's all we could ask.

It didn't help that people started putting towels over their heads when he came in to pitch. Curt Schilling did it some during the season. He started out doing it without thinking, but after a while other people picked up on it and it became, "I'll get on camera if I do this." A lot more people picked up on it for the World Series, and that's a shame, because all year long we talked about playing as a team and pulling for each other. Then you looked in the dugout and saw guys with towels over their heads. Managers say not to show them up. Umpires say not to show them up. We'll say the same thing to an opponent. And here some of our guys were showing up their own teammate. I think it's horseshit. If you can't watch, go back to the clubhouse.

I looked in our dugout in the ninth inning of the last game of the World Series, and I saw a guy with a towel over his head; I'm not going to mention any names, but I wanted so badly just to snatch that towel off his head and say, "Just pull for Mitch this one time. Wrap that damn towel around your neck and hang yourself if it's that painful." Jeez, if you don't want to watch, just go the hell home. We don't have a rule that you have to watch. Mitch getting into a jam is nothing new, but you should be pulling for him, not hiding your head like you can't bear to watch, like it's too scary or embarrassing or whatever. It's not like he had never had runners on first and second with one out in a one-run game before.

I don't feel sorry for Mitch. But I do think it's a shame that a couple of idiots who happened not to like his Wild Thing act could run him out of town. That's pretty much what happened, and it's not right.

I'm sure there are people in Philadelphia who don't like me. I'm sure there are people who don't like Darren Daulton or Lenny Dykstra or Dave Hollins. What if they called the front office and said, "We don't like them. We're going to kill them." What are they going to do? Get rid of all of us?

Now, I'm not saying it would have been easy for Mitch to come back. It would have been difficult. Real tough. The first time he walked a guy it would have been nasty. The fans would have been uncontrollable. But I also think that if there's one guy who could have handled it, it would have been Mitch. He's not going to change as a person, and he's not going to change the way he pitches. He's not going to go out there and tell himself, "Oh, my God, I can't walk this guy." He's going to put everything into every pitch he throws. If he walks him, he walks him. Then he'll try to get the next guy. One walk wouldn't bother him.

Somebody said it could have been a distraction for the team —and it might have been—to have a guy we're relying on to close out games for us who's being ridiculed by the fans. If he was a middle reliever, a guy who wouldn't get used much, maybe we could have worked around it. But he's the closer. If we have a lead of one, two, or three runs in the ninth, he's going to be in there. And if he blows it, things could get ugly. It's a touchy situation.

After he gave up the home run to Joe Carter, we had a few minutes with Mitch before the media got at him. Everyone went over and patted him on the back. We basically just said, "Forget about it. It's over. It could happen to anyone. What can you do?" You know, he could have gone into the back room and hid out and not faced the music when the media came in. But he faced the music and he sang the song. And no matter who you were on our team, even if you didn't like him or care for his act, you had to respect him right there. Because he showed a lot of class to stay in and answer all the questions.

I don't know what happened to him in the World Series. His velocity was down, I know that. All pitchers go through dead arm periods during the season. Mitch told me that's what he was going through, that his arm didn't hurt; it just didn't have any life in it. Maybe it was bad timing. But he pitched. He had the balls to go out there without close to his best stuff. He could have said he had a dead arm, that he couldn't pitch.

Of course, if he had, *I* might have had to pitch.

But that's the way it is with closers. When the game is on the line, they want the ball. If they didn't, you wouldn't want them. Here our season is on the line and he's going out there and he's told me he has a dead arm. But I wasn't too worried; he'd told me that before and then pitched great. I guess he was telling me the truth this time.

Another thing is, I don't know how much the death threats

affected him. I'm sure it had to. I read where Ed Rendell, the
mayor of Philadelphia, said it was no big deal, that he gets
death threats all the time, but I don't think that's the same
thing. The mayor has security people around him all the time.
Players are just sort of on their own, unprotected.

I can see why sometimes people would take Mitch wrong.
One of our starters would pitch a complete game and Mitch
would come into the clubhouse and throw his glove because
he wanted to pitch. There was a save opportunity and he
wanted to get it. Really, he's probably better suited to being an
everyday player. He needs to be out there.

Mitch always reacted well to constructive criticism. One day
he was pitching and it had been a long game. I was hot and
tired. It was the ninth inning and he came in and started walking guys. I went to the mound and said something like, "I want
to get the hell out of here. So if you don't stop walking all
these damn guys I'm going to fucking kill you." Or words to
that effect.

He looked at me and smiled and said, "I like it when you
yell at me."

They say left-handed pitchers are wacky and that you have
to be a little nuts to be a closer. So I guess that makes him
double bad.

I don't like what happened between Mitch and Curt Schilling. They didn't get along and that's fine, but then after Mitch
was traded they got into this horrible war of words in the press.
Mitch said he would throw at Curt if he faced him. Curt
said he wouldn't be the first one to the mound. That sort of
stuff.

Mitch is Mitch. Curt has been around him long enough to
know that Mitch is his own person, that he does his own thing.
Just let him be that way. We're all men. We should just worry
about ourselves.

He was a teammate. He went to battle for us. You don't

forget about all the things he did for us just because he gave up a home run. I'll never say a bad word about him.

I'll face Mitch sometime. But I faced him at his wildest, so that won't be the end of the world—but it's still going to be scary. I always told him that if I ever faced him I'd stand right on the plate. Because I knew he'd never hit me if I stood there.

I don't know who makes these schedules and decides what time we're going to play, but whoever it is just might be on some drugs we haven't heard of yet.

I'VE BEEN A BASEBALL FAN MOST OF MY life. When my family lived in New Jersey, we used to get all the Yankees games on television. They tell me that when I was young I used to sit on a wooden rocking horse and sing the national anthem. I thought it was the Yankee baseball song. They played it before all the Yankee games, right?

I've followed the game for a long time. Every once in a while somebody asks me one of those questions, like, If you could be commissioner for a day, what would you do? I just happen to have some thoughts.

Four strikes would be nice.

No stealing bases. If I can't do it, nobody should be allowed to.

In fact, just make everyone play at my speed. That would be fun.

If you advance a runner, it doesn't count against your batting average, just like a sacrifice.

Larry Walker can't try to throw people out at first base from right field when we play the Expos. If the ball goes through the infield, it's an automatic hit. That way you could jog to first.

Seriously, though, there are some things I don't like.

The first thing I would like to see is for them to go back to two divisions and get rid of that extra round of playoffs. I'll probably get in trouble for that one. Our owner, Bill Giles, was a big part of pushing through the new setup, but I don't think it's good.

It's going to be like hockey and football and basketball where it seems like every team makes the playoffs. You're going to have four teams in your league going to the playoffs. If they're going to do that, they should shorten the regular season.

Now, I know that's not going to happen. But the teams that make the playoffs and advance are going to end up playing too many games. And I'm not just talking as an everyday player; I'm thinking of the pitchers—for once. When it comes to the postseason, they sometimes have to pitch with two or three days' rest. That might be okay for two series, but if you add a third series it puts a lot of strain on a guy's arm and it could jeopardize his career. You don't want to see that.

A lot of players say they'd give their right arm to win a

World Series. I've probably said it myself. But I didn't mean it literally. Is it worth it? There are so many good young pitchers, you don't want to see one get blown up because he threw too many pitches in too short a time.

As I said before, if they want to make the playoffs longer, they should make the regular season shorter. The people who make these rules have never pitched. They've never played three-quarters of their games on artificial turf. They don't realize what a toll that takes. This probably isn't a good thing to say going into a year where I can be a free agent, but sometimes I think the owners have bigger egos than the players. That could force an early retirement for me, but I think it's the truth.

By the end of the World Series there wasn't a man on our team who would have been ready to play for another week or another series. Everybody was gassed. Everybody was done. If they're going to have all this extra stuff without shortening the season, I think some pitchers could go down. You hope not. But there are only so many pitches in an arm in a season. We're already on the brink; someone could snap and it would be ugly.

The guys who make the rules don't play, so they don't know what we go through. You wish there would come a point where they'd let the players in on some of these decisions. But of course we don't let those guys in on any of our decision-making either, so it's more or less screw you—screw them. But what can you do?

You read about how an owner in the NBA will consult one of his players about a decision that affects their team or about what's best for the league. Even their commissioner consults with the players. I guess if we had a commissioner, maybe he'd consult with the players. You never know. I think the owners like the way they have it now. They think they're in power—and come to think of it, they probably are.

I also think there's got to be a way to get rid of artificial turf. Look what happened to Moises Alou from Montreal; he was making a big turn at first and he tried to stop and his leg shattered. You have to think that if he had been running on dirt that wouldn't have happened.

I saw an Eagles game at the Vet early last season. A guy from the Bears planted and blew both his knees out without getting hit. The Phillies had an outfielder, Ron Jones, who looked like he was going to be a great hitter; he was coming in on a line drive, tried to stop, and ripped the patellar tendon in his knee. That probably wouldn't have happened on grass, and he would be playing somewhere today instead of being out of baseball.

I just think artificial turf is too hard on the body to play on it every day. I think we probably played 120 or 130 games on it last year. You just don't know how hurtful that is to your knees. And it's not just me. I'm overweight and it bothers my knees and back, but everyone says that they hurt if they play on it too much. Guys who come in from playing on a grass field notice the difference right away.

I know the artificial turf looks pretty on TV, and it can rain all day and you can still play on it that night. It's an economic thing. But you can also lose some valuable property, players you're paying a lot of money to, in the process.

I just think that there are enough smart people in the world who could invent some grass that would drain just as good as turf. Maybe they could even come up with some real grass that would grow inside the domed stadiums.

If they can't come up with indoor grass, just getting rid of the artificial turf in the outdoor stadiums would be a big help. I know the Phillies considered that a couple years ago. They said they couldn't do it because they have to convert the stadium between football and baseball. Maybe, but they've been doing it in San Diego for years. They have real grass, and the field is beautiful.

The owners say that real grass costs a lot of money. But what if one of their five-million-dollar ballplayers goes down with a knee injury and can't play anymore? Is the turf worth that kind of a loss? I don't think so.

I read where the Eagles brought in George Toma, the NFL's expert on fields, to look at the Vet. He said it was the worst playing surface in the league.

He was right. It's awful. It's the worst for baseball, too. There are a lot of hard spots. Where they paint the lines for football the turf is all matted down. It's so hard that it's like playing on concrete. Your spikes don't dig in. You see guys rounding first and they step on that hard spot and they slip. It's real dangerous.

When they convert the field for football, they put cutouts in where the bases and pitcher's mound are. The rest of the turf is real worn down, and the cutouts stick up because they're not worn down. That's got to be dangerous for the football players. Just like George Toma said, our turf is the worst in the league. You don't see as many bad hops on grass as you do at our place.

That isn't just an excuse for our fielding, by the way. Every player who comes in makes a comment about our turf. I think it was Terry Pendleton who asked during the playoffs if the warranty had run out on that rug. He said it was time to replace it, because someone was going to get seriously hurt. Some already have. I'd rather play on a bad grass field than a good turf field any day.

Here's another thing I'd like to change: now, I know a lot of people are going to disagree with me on this, but I don't like day games. It's too bright. If it's warm out, people wear a lot of white and light colors. They don't know how hard it is for us to see the ball against all those whites.

Every stadium has lights. Why not use them? Outfielders get much better jumps on fly balls at night than they do during the day.

If we have to play some day games, at least we should never have to play them to open a series the day after we've played a night game somewhere else. That happened to us last year. We played a night game in Los Angeles, then a day game in San Francisco the next day. There are rules in the Basic Agreement about that, but they don't count if the flight lasts less than a certain amount of time, or if it's the last trip, or if there's a makeup game involved. Lots of things can happen that make for tough scheduling.

Now, the Giants have gone with a lot of day games the last couple years and you can understand that, considering how miserable it is in San Francisco at night. But even a night game at Candlestick would have been better than what we had to do.

I'm sure somebody thought, Well, Los Angeles to San Francisco, that's not too long far. That's not too long a flight. But again, that's somebody who has never had to do it.

You have to remember that there might be a rain delay. There might be extra innings. The flight could be delayed or canceled. Things don't always run smoothly. Maybe they thought it would be a nice quick game and a nice quick flight and we'd get plenty of rest. Well, our team doesn't play quick games.

Here's what actually happened: We played at Dodger Stadium on a Wednesday night. There were no rain delays, no extra innings. The game lasted less than three hours. It ended before ten-thirty.

It takes about an hour for everybody to shower and get dressed and pack. Meanwhile they have to load up all the equipment. It's a pretty long drive from the stadium to the airport. So it was well after midnight before we got on the plane, but we couldn't take off right away because they still had to load the baggage and the equipment. Finally, we flew to San Francisco. By the time we landed, got onto the buses, and got to our hotel, it was close to three o'clock in the morning.

The first pitch was in ten hours and we were just getting to our rooms. As if the Giants pitching wasn't tough enough without all this help. We got one run on five hits and lost the game.

Then we played a night game on Friday. Why couldn't we have played Thursday night instead? Then we could have gotten some rest. I don't know who makes these schedules and decides what time we're going to play, but whoever it is just might be on some drugs we haven't heard of yet.

Some of these things are done for television, because that's where the money comes from. I understand that. It's kind of sad, really, that when you talk about baseball these days you end up talking about money so much.

The owners want a salary cap. I don't know. They say it works in basketball, but there are only twelve guys there, and it seems to me they run through some loopholes to get around it, too.

In baseball, a salary cap would be a big headache. For a twenty-five-man roster, it would cut out a lot of the extra players. There would be veterans making a lot of money, and there would be rookies. There would be nobody in between. It takes some guys three or four years to get settled in, so they could be gone before they have the chance to get really acclimated to the whole scene, unless they were willing to play for a lot less money. And I don't think they should be asked to do that; I'm a firm believer that the owners wouldn't pay us what they do if they couldn't afford it.

On a different subject, it seems like more guys go on the disabled list every year. I'm not sure why, but it probably has to do with money. There's that word again.

If a pitcher is making four million dollars a year and he feels a little twinge in his elbow, are you going to just sit around and wait five days to see if he can pitch? And if he can't, are you going to wait a sixth day or a seventh? No, you're probably just going to throw him on the disabled list and bring up somebody who's completely healthy. You don't want the pitcher to say he's all right and then go out and blow his arm out because the injury was worse than he thought. I think teams are more cautious now, especially with pitchers, because of all the money they're being paid. It's tough enough to find good pitchers. Teams want to keep what they've got.

Some fans think that today's players aren't tough and that they'd rather go on the disabled list than play with a few aches and pains. I'll admit there are guys like that. You see guys with a little something wrong and all of a sudden it's, "Oh, I'm hurt. I can't play." They think about how they're going to be a free agent and they don't want to hurt their statistics, so they go on the disabled list instead of toughing it out. They're just being selfish, and yes, there are players like that.

That's what I liked about the Phillies last year: I don't think we had anyone like that. Look at Dave Hollins. He played a couple weeks with a broken bone in his wrist; he wouldn't get it checked because he didn't want to find out. He told them for two or three weeks that his wrist was fine; he could hardly swing the bat, but he kept telling them, "Sure, I can play. Nothing wrong with me." Finally, when he couldn't swing anymore, the surgeons cut out a piece of bone and said he'd be out for four to six weeks. He was back in the lineup two weeks later.

It's all a matter of attitude. Dave wasn't 100 percent, but he wanted to play. He could have stayed on the disabled list. But times like that show what you have inside. There are some guys who can't tolerate any pain whatsoever, and there are other guys it doesn't bother at all.

They pay us to play baseball. I'd feel guilty if I had to sit out a whole year with an injury, no matter how bad it was, but I'd feel even worse to go on the disabled list just because I didn't feel exactly right—like if I had a little strain or something.

Baseball is a game of adjustments; if you can't adjust to a little ache or pain, if you have to go on the disabled list, there's something wrong with you. We play so many games that you're going to be sore a lot of the time. You're going to hurt. And if you can't tolerate that, I don't think I want you for my teammate.

We had a talk early last season, and we decided that we couldn't afford injuries. Guys who were hurt got rode hard. Pete Incaviglia hurt his knee; he got rode hard and he came back a little quicker than he probably should have. If you're hurt or on the disabled list, it's like you've got the plague or something. Nobody talks to you.

Our attitude was that if you get hurt, you get hurt. Hurry back, though, because we needed everyone we had. But when you have one guy playing hurt, it becomes contagious. How can you ask for a day off for a little pulled muscle or something when you look over at Dave Hollins? He's got stitches and they break open. The incision is bleeding and he's taping it up and going back out there. You think, "Shit, if he can play with that, I sure as hell can play with this." You might miss a game or two when it normally would have been four or five. And with the kind of money we make, I think we owe the team a full effort.

It seems like it always comes back to the money. I'm the first to say that the money we get paid is unbelievable. But that's the market right now, and you can't fault a guy for wanting to get what he deserves.

Sure, there's an ego thing that gets involved. You have to have an ego to play baseball, or any sport. Actors and actresses, they all have egos, too. If you think you're better than someone else, you think you should be making more money than he does. That's true in any job. But it does get to the point where it's hard to comprehend. If somebody puts $3 million in your pocket and $200,000 falls out, you're not going to miss it too much. That's weird and it's scary, but that's the way I look at it.

When I first came up I thought $60,000 was all the money in the world. Then I said, man, if I could just make $1 million for one year I could quit and never have to worry about anything again. Then I started thinking that if I ever made $2 million, my brothers could retire, too, and we could just play golf every day.

Those are my goals right now: to help the Phillies win and to help my brothers out so we can play a lot of golf. We make a helluva foursome. Might have to buy our own course, because it's possible nobody else would let us on theirs. Not if they're smart.

I still don't realize how much I've made. Don't grasp it. My agent, Davis Burk, keeps me on a budget. I see the bank statements every month, but he's a tight man. I feel guilty asking for my own money. Once I had to borrow $500 from Pete Incaviglia just to get through a road trip. Maybe I'll realize it all after I've retired and they tell me I don't have to do anything else and I can be real lazy.

Whenever people talk about what's good for baseball, the designated hitter rule comes up eventually. I'm glad the National League doesn't have it.

I mean, it's good in a way. It helps out some guys who are getting a little older and might not be as good in the field as they used to be, but they can still swing the bat. Guys like Dave Winfield and Paul Molitor and Harold Baines—they can still do what they do best. You like to see that Andre Dawson is still able to go out there and play.

People will come to games to see people hit. There may only be one or two guys people will come to watch field—Ozzie Smith, maybe Chico Lind. People want to see pitching and they want to see hitting, so I guess the DH helps in that way.

But I think it hurts, too. The pitchers don't have to hit, so they're more apt not to care about throwing at the batter. If a pitcher has to hit, he's going to think twice about knocking somebody on his ass, knowing the same thing could happen to him when he comes up. Of course, a lot of pitchers don't hit that well, so if the game is for the fans, do they really want to pay to watch pitchers hit? It's not pretty. Still, I don't like the designated hitter rule.

Now, a designated runner . . .

Aw, just kidding. But I really don't like the DH. It takes away from the strategy, and I think it tends to wear down pitchers. In the American League, if it's a 4–4 game in the sixth inning, the starter is probably going to still be in there. In the National League, same situation, he's probably coming out for a pinch-hitter.

That doesn't mean, of course, that if a few years from now some American League team offered me a job as a designated hitter that I wouldn't do it. I would. I don't think anybody would want me to, but I think I could. I'm not real fond of fielding, you know. It's that old lumber-or-leather thing. Bill Madlock told me once that, if you shake a tree, ten gloves will fall out but only one bat. I didn't get here because of my nimble feet in the field.

I think I could be a DH. It would depend on the situation. If I felt like I couldn't play the field anymore but I still wanted to keep playing, yeah, I'd be interested if somebody wanted me. On the other hand, if my knees hurt too bad to play the field, they would probably hurt too bad to run the bases, too.

I've talked to some of the players who have come to the National League from the American League. They say how bad some of the ballparks are, so old. But I might like to play in that league one year. It would be fun to see what Fenway Park is like. It would be nice to play in Yankee Stadium, where I used to go as a kid. That would be fun. Tiger Stadium, Detroit.

Yankee Stadium, SkyDome in Toronto, and Baltimore's Camden Yards—that's it for the American League parks I've been to. I've also seen Memorial Stadium in Baltimore where the Orioles used to play. I used to watch Eddie Murray play there when I was a kid. I tell him that all the time. It pisses him off.

One thing that's changed since I began playing is the strength of the American League. When I started, the National League was dominant. We won the All-Star game almost every year and usually the World Series, too. But now they've got so many young bombers in the American League—Ken Griffey, Jr., and Juan Gonzalez, and guys like that. Jeez, it's like they've got football players over there. Big, strong guys who can run, too.

What happened, I think, was that for a while, the National League had bigger parks and more artificial turf, so teams adapted by getting smaller, faster guys who could cover a lot of ground in the outfield. But guys like that usually don't have a lot of power. Some of the guys in the American League are scary, they're so huge. I just look at them and say, "Thank God I'm in the other league." The home run hitting contest at the All-Star game? Couldn't watch it.

Right now I think the American League has better players. These things go in phases, though. In a few years I think it will turn around again and the National League will get back on top.

**He may be President, but he's not
pardoned from being ragged on.
If I can get on Dale Murphy, I can
rag Bill Clinton.**

WE WERE GOING TO HAVE A PARADE
down Broad Street in Philadelphia if we had won the World
Series. Joe Carter's home run canceled that. Among other
things.

What they decided to do instead was to have a ceremony in
front of City Hall a couple of weeks later. I didn't know what

kind of crowd to expect, since we hadn't won it all. The Eagles were off to a great start by that time, and a lot of our guys had gone their separate ways. We thought it was really too late. Who was going to be there?

The turnout was unbelievable.

Jim Fregosi and Darren Daulton came in from Florida to be there. Lenny Dykstra and Curt Schilling and Kevin Stocker showed up. Bill Giles and Lee Thomas. I drove in from West Virginia.

I was a little reluctant to go at first. I thought it was a stupid idea and that no one would show up. But it was really impressive. It shows you that the Phillies fans, no matter what, will get behind you if they know you played hard. The majority of them, anyway.

I was glad I went. They pulled the big Phillies hat off the statue of Billy Penn and presented it to the team, so I finally got to see it in person. There was a huge billboard signed by fans thanking us for the season. It was really nice. It had been such a long year, such a roller-coaster ride. And then when the roller coaster stopped, it stopped right at the bottom. I was like, Man, I don't even want to think about next year. I don't want to think about any of it.

But then, when I saw the way the fans reacted, it was like getting a new life. You start wondering when spring training is going to start. I went home and told my wife to start looking for a place in Florida, call somebody, let's get going. I was all excited. It made me feel like I was ready to go out and pick up a ball and a bat right then.

Of course, the urge passed when something good came on television.

Philadelphia fans, though, can give you energy. As you get older, you need all the help you can get, and that ceremony was a real kick. I had been telling people at home that I had been to the All-Star game, been to the World Series, that's it,

I'm done; I was so tired I didn't want to play the next year. But I stopped thinking that way after that little ceremony.

Harry Kalas was up there introducing everybody, giving a little speech. He said, "Darren Daulton for mayor!" Everybody cheered. I guess Harry liked that. So he said, "John Kruk for president!" They cheered again.

Unfortunately I had to decline the nomination. I've got enough problems just waking up every morning and getting out of bed to be thinking about running the country. The country's got enough problems, too.

But I have to admit that some of us had thought about what it would be like if we won the World Series and got invited to the White House. It seems like lately every team that wins goes to the Rose Garden to meet the President and have their picture taken.

I think that would have been great. I would have had a lot of fun with that, because of the way Bill Clinton made fun of my hair. After he got in that mess for supposedly paying two hundred dollars for a haircut, he made fun of my hair; he said, "How about that guy who plays first base for the Phillies? Who do you think cuts his hair?"

I would have had fun with that. What the hell? Clinton's a human being, just like the rest of us. He's done some good things, but he's made some mistakes, too. Like the rest of us. He may be President, but he's not pardoned from being ragged on.

I'll put it this way: if I can get on Dale Murphy, I can rag Bill Clinton. I hold Murf in a lot higher esteem than any president. To me, Murf has the seat right below God. Bill Clinton is probably down here with the rest of us.

I think it would have been fun to go to the White House, though. It's hard to tell what I would have said, but I'm sure I would have come up with something. The first thing I probably would have asked him is why in the hell did he raise our taxes?

To me, it doesn't make sense. You get punished for being successful. You've got a skill, you work hard to become one of the best in your profession, and you're penalized for that.

It's funny how things turn out. Early in the season, we were in first place. So the outside media started coming to see what we were all about. And we started getting all this notoriety. They would walk into our clubhouse and we'd be playing cards. And maybe you lose a hand and you're leaning over and slapping Larry Bowa on the back of the head, or he's hitting you. And Pete Incaviglia is running around, screaming the way he does, with no shirt on, looking like Godzilla.

And they thought, "Well, these guys are crazy." And they jumped on that and took it a lot further than we thought it would go. But the story went there. And it was true.

Yeah, we have some crazy people. And we have some guys with long hair, and some of us probably don't shave as often as we should, and a couple of us could maybe stand to lose a couple pounds. But we were a good team. We knew how to play the game. And when we read the articles later, it seemed that those things kind of got pushed aside. The whole article would be about how we don't bathe, how we don't shave, how we don't cut our hair, how we yell and curse and scream and fight with each other. And then the last line might be, like, Oh, by the way, they're also a pretty good team.

At first it kind of pissed us off. After a while, though, we decided that if that's what they wanted to write about, let's really get it going. That's when we started telling them stuff like that we don't use deodorant, haven't taken a shower in weeks, that kind of stuff.

I think that's one of the reasons the front office never called down and said we should get a haircut or shave or whatever. I don't think they liked all that stuff at first, but then they realized how much notoriety it gave us and they jumped on it. Then they were happy for us to be renegades and lowlifes and dirtbags. I think the legend got bigger than it should have, but what are you going to do?

Even in the playoffs and the World Series, that was all anybody wanted to talk about. But when you think about the Phillies, you should disregard the long hair and the facial hair and instead remember that we played the game the way it's supposed to be played. We played hard. We broke up double plays. We moved the runners. We scored runs without getting a hit. We never gave up. We battled. We believed in ourselves. The only thing that upset me about all that other stuff was that people overlooked one thing: we were really a damn good baseball team.

I have no complaints, though. I've had a lot of fun in baseball. It's like Andy Van Slyke said once—that he felt like a guy who drove the Budweiser truck into the stadium, snuck into a closet, put on a uniform, and just stuck around and played.

That's the way I feel. I think of all these guys. I think about the way I felt when I met Nolan Ryan. The way I felt when I met Wade Boggs. Nolan Ryan is larger than life, not just in the baseball world but in all sports. He's up there with Michael Jordan and the rest.

Of course, there are times when reality hits you and hits you hard. I guess by now most people have heard about my little medical problem. Sometimes I feel like I'm the most famous one-testicled man around right now.

It all started last July in Los Angeles. Mitch Williams fielded a swinging bunt and turned and fired, and the ball kind of hit the wet grass and bounced up and hit me in the testicles. It broke my cup. I swelled up, but I thought that was all it was. I guess we found out it was more than that.

I didn't treat it the way I should. I should have checked on it, but I didn't. I just kind of ignored it and hoped it would go away.

Then, over the winter, I noticed a lump had formed. But

still, I never got it checked. I kept waiting and waiting. Then, when I got to Florida and started doing stuff, running and wearing my cup again, taking ground balls, and all that, I kept irritating it more and more. So I decided it was time to get it checked—which is what people had been telling me all winter. I kept ignoring them, though. Stubborn. Stupid.

Jamie had a lot to do with me finally going in and doing it. I was complaining all the time about the pain. I think she got tired of listening to me. I finally just gave in, maybe just to keep her off my back.

When the lump got bigger, I knew something was wrong. I just waited too long. And it cost me. Not just my right testicle, but it meant I could miss part of the season.

I told our team doctor, Phillip Marone, to check it when we had our physicals at the beginning of spring training. I told him that I had a lump, so he checked and he immediately set up an appointment. Good thing I told him, because he doesn't usually check for that. He checks for a hernia, but he doesn't check for bumps and stuff. I don't blame him at all for that; I never really wanted a doctor rolling my testicles around in his hand. You should do that on your own.

I had an ultrasound examination. That was a fun experience. They said there was some abnormality there. And I said, "What could it be?" And they said it might just be where it was bleeding from the trauma of being hit. It could have just dried and formed a hematoma. Then I said, "What's the worst case scenario?" And they told me, "Cancer."

That's when I started thinking about it and worrying about it. But even when I went back to Philadelphia for more tests and the surgery, they thought it was just a hematoma. They said there was a chance it was cancer, but they didn't think it was. And even if it was cancer, it had nothing to do with getting hit by Mitch's throw.

They were talking about just treating it with some antibiotics and some anti-inflammatory medication for a couple weeks, and then, if it got better, they were going to leave it at that. If it didn't, then they were going to remove it and test it.

I thought about it. But two weeks was too long to wait, because then, if they had to take it out, it would be three weeks after that before I could play, and I definitely would have missed some of the season. So all of us agreed it would be best to just take it out. They did, and that's when they found the cancer.

And then I had to talk about it. That was more embarrassing than anything. Who wants to talk about their nuts in public? Who wants to go around telling people you only have one testicle? It's not easy to do.

But I think to go through this with this team is going to be a lot easier than it would be to go through it if I didn't play sports. Because they're going to let me know that I have one testicle. They're going to make jokes about it. I'm sure that on the plane somebody's going to hand me a bag of peanuts and say, "Here's an extra one." Stuff like that.

My first day back in the clubhouse Larry Andersen had a good one. Mitch had sent me a basket that had a bunch of fruit and crackers and nuts and stuff. And he said, "I don't know if he's going to like the fruit, but I know he'll appreciate the nuts."

I expect to hear a lot of that from the players. And I know I'll hear it from fans in other cities. I'm sure in Chicago they're going to give me some shit about it. No stone goes unturned with the bleacher bums. But the abuse I take there won't be anything compared to the abuse I'm going to take from my teammates.

I made a lot of jokes about it when I had to talk about it. I said I wished I had taken care of it over the winter because then I wouldn't have to be standing there talking about my private parts, that I felt like Howard Stern. Stuff like that. But it was just because I was embarrassed and nervous, so I had to joke about it.

But the good thing is that, with all the publicity it's gotten, maybe some men will check now. They can save themselves from a lot of grief if they'll just check.

When you're an athlete, you don't accept defeat. This isn't defeat, but it's a big stumbling block. Whenever you hear cancer, you always think the worst. The best way for me to accept it is to joke about it. I know some people probably thought I was making fun of cancer while there are little kids dying from it. But I'm not making fun of cancer. That's a serious thing. It's just the way I handle it. And cancer's not always a death sentence. It's good for people to realize that.

Mitch called me right after it was over. He said that when they read all the stories about how if it hadn't been for him they never would have found the cancer, he went into the Astros clubhouse and they were all high-fiving him for saving my life.

He said he kind of felt strange about it. He said he felt like he went from being the biggest asshole in Philadelphia, because of the World Series and the early stories that his throw had caused the problem, to probably being a hero.

In my book, he's a hero. I never thought I'd say it, but now I couldn't be happier that Mitch made that throw. What can you say when the best thing that ever happened to you is getting hit in the nuts?

From now on, when I think about Mitch, I won't think about those blown saves in the World Series. Turns out he was responsible for the biggest save of my life.